MEXICANS IN REVOLUTION, 1910–1946

The Mexican Experience

William H. Beezley, series editor

MEXICANS IN REVOLUTION 1910–1946

AN INTRODUCTION

WILLIAM H. BEEZLEY &
COLIN M. MACLACHLAN

UNIVERSITY OF NEBRASKA PRESS · LINCOLN & LONDON

∞

Library of Congress Cataloging-
in-Publication Data
Mexicans in revolution, 1910–1946 : an
introduction / William H. Beezley and
Colin M. MacLachlan.
p. cm. — (The Mexican experience)
Includes bibliographical references and
index.
ISBN 978-0-8032-2447-6 (pbk. : alk.
paper)
1. Mexico—History—Revolution,
1910–1920. 2. Mexico—History—
1910–1946. 3. Mexico—Politics and
government—1910–1946. I. MacLachlan, Colin M. II. Title.
F1234.B39 2009
972.08'16—dc22
2008052431

Set in Adobe Garamond.

CONTENTS

ILLUSTRATIONS

ACKNOWLEDGMENTS

The Mexican generation who made the world's first social revolution by defeating the regime of Porfirio Díaz and carrying out a critical social campaign for three decades has fascinated us for years. We have undertaken this concise history to incorporate new interpretations of the movement, provide an appreciation of the revolution as the nation approaches its centennial in 2010, and to respond to the scholarly disregard for revolutionary achievements. In recent years we have watched with dismay the dismissal of this revolutionary experience through the application of the misnomer "postrevolutionary" to the dynamic, essential programs during the years 1920–1946. (See "Reflections on the Historiography of Twentieth-Century Mexico," *History Compass* 5, no. 3 [May 2007]: 963–74.) We want this volume to restore vitality to the study of the revolutionaries and their programs.

Colleagues and friends have contributed to our interpretation of these revolutionaries and their programs. Here we cannot thank all those who have contributed to our interpretations. We intend to thank them in person, if possible. We acknowledge those who have made an immediate impact on this work. For help with photographs we want to thank Cheryle Champion, the Marmolejo family, and Terri Grant at the El Paso Library. We express our gratitude to Ricardo Pérez Montfort, Carmen Nava, and Guillermo Palacios in Mexico City; Angela

Villalba, Elena Albarrán, Amanda López, Gretchen Pierce, Ageeth Sluis, Monica Rankin, Heather Lundine, and Bridget Barry in the United States.

We dedicate this book to the memory of Michael C. Meyer and, as always, to Blue.

MEXICANS IN REVOLUTION, 1910–1946

States and Territories
★ Capital
Aguascalientes — Aguascalientes
Baja California — Mexicali
Baja California Sur — La Paz
Campeche — Campeche
Coahuila — Saltillo
Colima — Colima
Chiapas — Tuxtla Gutiérrez
Chihuahua — Chihuahua
Distrito Federal — (national capital)
Durango — Durango
Guerrero — Chilpancingo
Guanajuato — Guanajuato
Hidalgo — Pachuca
Jalisco — Guadalajara
Michoacán — Morelia
Morelos — Cuernavaca
México — Toluca
Nayarit — Tepic
Nuevo León — Monterrey
Oaxaca — Oaxaca
Puebla — Puebla
Quintana Roo — Chetumal
Querétaro — Querétaro
Sinaloa — Culiacán
San Luis Potosí — San Luis Potosí
Sonora — Hermosillo
Tabasco — Villahermosa
Tlaxcala — Tlaxcala
Tamaulipas — Ciudad Victoria
Veracruz — Xalapa
Yucatán — Mérida
Zacatecas — Zacatecas
N
BAJA CALIFORNIA
BAJA CALIFORNIA SUR
SONORA
CHIHUAHUA
COAHUILA
NUEVO LEÓN
TAMAULIPAS
SINALOA
DURANGO
ZACATECAS
SAN LUIS POTOSÍ
AGUAS-CALIENTES
NAYARIT
GUANAJUATO
QUERÉTARO
HIDALGO
TLAXCALA
JALISCO
MÉXICO
D.F.
MORELOS
PUEBLA
VERACRUZ
COLIMA
MICHOACÁN
GUERRERO
OAXACA
TABASCO
CHIAPAS
CAMPECHE
YUCATÁN
QUINTANA ROO
0 100 200 300 Miles

INTRODUCTION

Changing Times and Generations

Small bands of Mexicans initiated the world's first popular social revolution on November 20, 1910. These revolutionaries represented a cross section of ethnic and age groups, and came from all walks of life and levels of society. Nevertheless, for the majority of them, age and regional origins, more than class, employment, or ethnicity, stood out as their most striking characteristics. Despite a substantial number of young women, young single men from small provincial towns dominated the revolutionary forces. Some revolutionaries quickly learned the necessary military tactics, political strategies, and personal skills to survive, even to flourish. Slow learners perished or fled to Europe or the United States. Those who remained, perhaps as a result of vacancies created by death and exile, became the leaders who established significant national reforms. As a generation, they shaped the destiny of their nation across the twentieth century.

The revolutionaries, in general, were passionate about their compatriots to the point of death, optimistic to the point of being foolhardy, ambitious to the point of being reckless, and desperate to the point of having nothing to lose. Each of these characteristics had its origin in the successful programs of national development that had occurred in the previous regime under the direction of Porfirio Díaz. Proud of the nation's accomplishments, aware of opportunities, eager for success, and dismayed that they had not shared equitably in the nation's burgeoning agricultural, mining, and industrial profits, these revolutionaries as a generation intended to open possibilities not only for themselves, but also for all Mexicans.

The revolutionaries fought for control of the nation, at first against members of the previous regime and then among themselves, in order to carry out initiatives to create a government responsive to the people, putting first the needs of the citizens, and controlling its own natural and human resources. They attempted to mold a new generation that would continue the revolution's efforts for the people into the future. Their campaigns included programs for land reform, worker protection, widespread literacy, and mandatory schools. They sought a better life with adequate housing, sufficient food, and public health measures, while eliminating the social, cultural and political intrusions of the Catholic Church and ending the hostility, prejudice, and brutality toward indigenous and poor Mexicans. Throughout the entire period they endured high levels of violence. As individuals, these young men claimed top military ranks, occupied leading political positions, demanded economic profits, and assumed elite social positions, often by marrying well. At the same time that they personally benefited, throughout the era from 1910–1946 this generation of revolutionaries sought to restore national honor by demanding respect from foreigners and pride from Mexicans of every class, gender, or ethnicity.

The revolutionaries shared unanimous commitment to the people and common dedication to national changes, but they disputed the priority of necessary reforms. Violence served as their idiom of discussion, resulting in a civil war in 1915 and 1916 in the midst of revolution, and periodic rebellions throughout the era. Each major leader hammered out an agenda for reform that reflected the ambitions of his followers and his personal visions for their region and the nation. These statements of goals were shaped by the experiences of individuals and by the historical context of local communities. All of the plans for revolutionary changes reflected the successes and, at times, the excesses of the regime that preceded the revolution.

The Porfirian Context of Revolution

The roots of the Revolution reached back to the successful programs of the government of Porfirio Díaz and his regime, called the Porfiriato, that governed the republic from 1876 to 1911. This administration completed the national recovery from the French Intervention (the era of French occupation and constant fighting against them and Conservatives by Liberals led by Benito Juárez, 1862–1867) through the construction of social stability eliminating endemic banditry and political rebellions. Under these peaceful conditions, Díaz revived and expanded the national economy, generally raising the levels of prosperity in the nation. This administration introduced changes that commercialized agriculture, modernized mining, financed industries, initiated railroads, and enticed consumers. The national programs created substantial profits that resulted in increased prosperity in general, but they did so in a dramatically uneven manner. A few individuals obtained substantial profits, while the majority did not. A combination of opportunities brought advantages to those able to adjust to the new enterprises. At the same time, these economic changes exposed a large segment of the population to demands that they did not understand nor could they meet in positive and productive ways.

Agriculturists shifted from subsistence to commercial crops with a market in the cities, Europe, or the United States. The change required practices that included the economies of scale, widespread irrigation, and mechanical processing, with labor demands that conflicted with customary practices. The transfer of land titles characterized the changes in agriculture and the amount of property converted from traditional village ownership to new commercial enterprises during the Porfiriato amounted to an astonishing 127,111,824 acres—well over half of the nation's arable lands. The owners of what today would be called agribusinesses seized the most fertile lands, conveniently located with access to both water and transportation. Mining, invigorated with new technology that made it more efficient, responded to a broader world market and new demands in both the United States and Europe. Railways extended markets beyond national borders. Labor contractors reached beyond regional pools to the nation as a whole. By the 1880s, workers even traveled along the rail network into the American Southwest. Textile, cigarette, and preserved food industries adopted the latest mechanical technology and inspired the beginnings of a modern working class. Set hours, repetitive tasks, and cash wages demanded adjustments that altered village life for workers who hovered psychologically between the industrial production and subsistent agriculture. Across the nation, available new products and imaginative business promotions together with an increasing number of individuals relying on wages and others with growing discretionary incomes combined to form expanding consumer markets in staple and luxury goods. The result was the rise of an elite society that even included members of the middle class that adopted cosmopolitan fashions and diversions, including opera and sports.

Porfirian officials favored monopoly concessions as a means of attracting foreign capital to assume unknown risks, offering the hope of recouping the investment and the prospect of lavish rewards in a protected market. Railroad concessions had set the pattern as early as the government of Antonio López de Santa Anna in 1853–1855, although little actual rail construction took place under this first contract. During the Porfiriato, as railroad construction dominated popular attention, city residents also witnessed the introduction of additional technology, such as gas lighting, tramlines, and other advances often of cosmopolitan origins. Railroads quickly began hauling raw materials to the United States or to ports for shipment to Europe. Foreigners enticed to invest received generous terms that in retrospect seemed excessive, and their presence in high-profile projects obscured the participation of Mexicans in the process. Although bankruptcies abounded in the early days as foreigners failed to appreciate local obstacles or gauge the domestic and international markets, by the late 1880s foreign investors reaped amazing profits.

Ordinary Mexicans, who supplied the labor and raw materials, marveled that the future appeared mortgaged to foreigners. The trick was to assure that monopoly concessions did not reach a point that closed opportunities for the domestic entrepreneurs and excessively exploited domestic workers. Commercial crops and railroad development swept across the country, resulting in the new towns of Torreón and Gómez Palacios and a mobile population of workers who labored in mines, built railroads, cut timber, and went home to grow crops.

In Mexico City, the past rubbed against the future, with the rich sequestered in the western neighborhoods with wide boulevards, modern houses, and fancy stores carrying all the latest items from Paris, New York, and London. In the eastern parts of the city ambitious peasants and poor workers lived amid the decaying, abandoned colonial buildings without sewers and only minimal access to potable water. During the rainy season mud and filth flowed together to create almost impassable streets and conditions ripe for disease. Infant mortality, nutritional problems, and premature death characterized the lot of this population.

The poor sometimes went hungry. The switch to commercial crops at times resulted in food shortages. Production dropped of beans, corn, and chili, the staples of the national diet, requiring the importation of corn for tortillas from the United States during bad harvests. Riots occurred in scattered locations throughout the republic during the period from 1900 to 1910. In the worst year, 1907, both commercial agriculture and mining slumped. Per capita corn production fell by 50 percent in 1907 from its 1877 level. Unemployed miners in the north roamed the streets. Workers left their jobs to protest wages and conditions at both the Cananea Consolidated Copper Company in Sonora and the Rio Blanco textile mills in Veracruz. They remained off the job until President Díaz ordered the military to break both strikes. These desperate conditions resulted from both national economic policies and international market depression.

During these years of economic disruption, national progress seemed threatened by the lack of vigorous leadership. As he aged,

Díaz turned to a smaller and smaller circle of younger, technocratic advisors, rather than developing a system of political recruitment. Increasing discomfort with the octogenarian Díaz's unwillingness to provide for an orderly transition troubled the political, economic, and social elites. The president's concession to allow the selection of a vice president (1904) resulted in the elevation of Ramón Corral, who was widely judged to be an unacceptable successor because of his ruthless policies against the Yaqui Indians in Sonora. The unwillingness of Díaz to deal seriously with the succession process alienated individuals, but most of them hid their opposition to his continuation in office behind customary smiles.

The journalist Ricardo Flores Magón became the most outspoken critic of the president's continuation in office, the small circle of political advisors occupying administrative positions, and the unimaginative and anti-labor economic politics. He and his brother Enrique organized the Mexican Liberal Party (PLM) that demanded an end to the Porfirian political and economic regime and a return to the liberalism of Benito Juárez. Facing government repression, the PLM fled first to San Antonio, Texas, and then St. Louis, Missouri, where in 1906, Flores Magón called for revolution, as his politics moved further toward anarchism. Eventually he was arrested by U.S. marshals, for violation of the century-old neutrality legislation, and after more than a decade of incarceration he died in the federal prison in Leavenworth, Kansas. Flores Magón became a symbol of anarchist resistance to both U.S. and Mexican industrial suppression of Mexican workers. Today he is recognized as a champion by the Chicano movement in the United States and by unions in Mexico.

Other opponents, including several talented and qualified individuals, wanted to replace President Díaz, but hesitated to confront the man who had become an icon of national progress. Journalist James Creelman's interview of Díaz for *Pearson's Magazine* in 1908 added even more uncertainty. In the course of the interview, the president indicated that he encouraged the formation of political parties, because he did not intend to be a candidate for the presidency in 1910. His statement set off a flurry of excitement across the nation, while the president himself focused on the centennial year of independence. He planned a celebration to demonstrate to the world that Mexico under his rule had become a modern country. It represented both a celebration of the man and what the world saw as his personal creation. The remarkable progress of the nation, presented to an audience ready to be impressed, obscured the reality that time had run out for the Porfirians.

Different kinds of candidates began to consider the presidential elections based on their convictions of how to preserve the international reputation, social tranquility, and economic expansion achieved by the Díaz regime. In the northeastern state of Nuevo León, General Bernardo Reyes believed that the Porfirian success rested on having a veteran military officer at the top. In the Veracruz region, General Félix Díaz, nephew of the president, proposed to continue the regime's longevity by having another Díaz family member as president. In Sonora, vice president and governor Ramón Corral found the Porfirian success in tough-minded administration, such as that of a frontier governor. In the capital city, the Científicos believed that the social application of technology had maintained the regime, but remained uncertain of the individual candidate.

Two additional opinions on the actions necessary to preserve Porfirian achievements and arrange a smooth transition of authority appeared in book form. In Mexico City, the intellectual Andrés Molina Enríquez focused on commercial agricultural expansion with concomitant land consolidation of the 1890s as the greatest danger to the nation because it stripped property from small, subsistence farmers and reduced staple crop production. Molina Enríquez did not envision himself a presidential candidate, but his conclusions expressed in *Los Grandes Problemas Nacionales* became guiding principles for land reform programs for the first half of the twentieth century.

In Coahuila, Francisco, the youngest son of the powerful but ignored Madero family, stated in his widely circulated book on the presidential selection that the preservation of Porfirian successes would only be possible with the peaceful transfer of presidential power and that this could only occur through democratic elections. His arguments in *La Succesión Presidencial en 1910* laid the basis for his presidential campaign.

A fractured society, a disgruntled, but silent elite, a desperate lower class, and a president who had ruled beyond his time marked the end of an era that took a decade to die (1901–1911). Most of the proponents of these different political positions acted with circumspection, waiting to see if indeed President Díaz had decided to step down. Within months, he allowed himself to be persuaded by various groups, including the circle of governors, to reverse his position and accept nomination for the presidency in the 1910 election. Lying in the weeds again allowed Corral to become the vice presidential nominee (a concession by the eighty-year-old Díaz that he might not survive an entire term) and enabled the Científicos and others to maintain their positions in the Porfirian inner circle. On the other hand, General Reyes, in his designs on his presidency, had gone beyond the chain of command. Díaz, in short order, had Reyes traveling the globe to review military modernization programs. This assignment meant he would lack the required year's residence within national borders before elections. The president ignored Madero, whose reputation as a dilettante agriculturalist and committed Spiritualist were believed to discredit him.

President Díaz focused his attention during the summer of 1910 on the celebration of the centennial of national independence. Centennial ceremonies, in a series of celebrations across the country, marked the initiation of the struggle, and throughout the summer various events drew the attention of both national and international audiences, building to a climax on Independence Day, September 16. In the middle of these events, the elections in July occurred without incident and government officials reported that Porfirio Díaz had been reelected with an overwhelming number of votes.

For Mexicans in general, but especially those in the capital city, the late summer of 1910 brought the inauguration of new buildings, monuments, and institutions (including an insane asylum) to commemorate independence. The grand national celebration was held on September 16, with parades and speeches that drew official and unofficial visitors from Europe, the United States, Latin America, and Asia, particularly Japan. The centennial parades highlighted the story of Mexico's past, through the stages of ancient Aztec glories, colonial civilizing efforts, and the Porfirian creation of a cosmopolitan nation. Through it all, the elderly president remained remote; the patriarchal patriot had seemingly become detached from daily activities, serving only as the national symbol. As the Díaz regime basked in the afterglow of the centennial celebrations, on November 20 insurrectionary battles erupted in distant Chihuahua and the revolution sputtered to life.

The first social revolution of the twentieth century had begun. The Russian, the Chinese, and the Cuban revolutions later lurched into existence in reaction to the old regimes in those countries. These revolutions drew on well-established socialist and subsequently communist philosophical responses to feudal, colonial, and imperial systems. Lenin, Mao, and Castro closed their societies behind the doors of ideology and promoted social changes driven by theories. The Mexican Revolution resulted from a decidedly different context and programs. The successes, not the failures, of the previous regime generated these revolutionaries. They took pride in their nation, its political stability, economic successes, and international reputation, but they wanted to share in its government, profits, and prestige. They recognized the opportunities for ambitious individuals and they wanted to see hard work and initiative rewarded. Once their struggle began, the revolutionaries eventually mobilized the majority of the nation's people in a campaign to make the good life lived by the Porfirian elites available to everyone. Despite staggering obstacles to implementing social changes (including the deaths of some two million individuals, about one in seven Mexicans), the revolutionaries never wavered in their commitment. Once in power they adopted an empirical, practical, nonideological projects (unless one counts anticlericalism as an ideology), open to the social experiments by others. They built their programs on cosmopolitan pragmatism devised by foreign travel and innovative improvisation based on wartime experiences. This generation willed into law, if not completely into everyday practice, what before them had been unimaginable: the creation of a just, equitable, and good life for all Mexicans.

Suggested Reading on the Porfirian Regime

Beezley, William H. *Judas at the Jockey Club*, revised ed. Lincoln: University of Nebraska Press, 2004.

Frank, Patrick. *Posada's Broadsheets: Mexican Popular Imagery, 1890–1910*. Albuquerque: University of New Mexico Press, 1998.

Garner, Paul H. *Porfirio Díaz: Profiles in Power*. New York: Longman's, 2001.

Johns, Michael. *The City of Mexico in the Age of Díaz*. Austin: University of Texas Press, 1997.

Schell, William, Jr. *Integral Outsiders: The American Colony in Mexico City, 1876–1911*. Wilmington DE: SR Books, 2001.

1

A GENERATION OF REBELS

(*Previous page*) 1. Photograph of the revolutionary dead. Nearly one in seven Mexicans died as a result of the revolutionary fighting during the decade from 1910 to 1920. Postcards and photographs recorded the deaths that scarred the nation. Photograph by Otis Aultman, used with the permission of the El Paso Public Library, El Paso, Texas.

Tidings of Revolution

Francisco Madero became a revolutionary by accident. His entire life—his family, his education, his marriage, and his early business efforts—marked him as a member of the elite. Madero's status rested on his family's connection with the Porfirian inner circle of promoters, but his prospects suffered because he came from the provinces, not the capital city. His frustrations serve as a microcosm of the growing exclusion of provincials from the political and economic opportunities of the Porfirian regime. These provincials had limited access to federal political power though their social world had broadened beyond their home states. Educated in Mexico City and in other countries, dressed in the latest fashions, and possessing the requisite wealth and appropriate manners, the provincials were indistinguishable from the capital city politicians and socialites except for their lack of a capital city accent and acceptance by the locals. They had everything except a Mexico City street address—though some even maintained weekend homes there. These disgruntled provincial leaders could have been drawn into the political system had Porfirio Diaz supported political parties. Sensitive to their exclusion, they had become an explosive potential; their shoddy treatment later came back to haunt Díaz and his capital city claque. In many ways Madero represented the least able of the disenchanted provincial elites: inferior in almost every way except the one that counted most, Madero possessed the crucial daring needed to challenge Díaz.

Madero launched a presidential campaign following the publication of the Creelman magazine interview in which Díaz announced that he believed Mexicans were ready for an open presidential race in 1910. Madero's friends and family, as well as many other Mexicans, believed that Madero's campaign was foolhardy if not suicidal. Nevertheless, he campaigned across the nation on the platform of no presidential reelection and developed a following that recognized his courage in entering politics. His organizational efforts, especially the organization of the Anti-reelectionist Party, eventually seemed a little too successful to Díaz, who had Madero arrested on trumped-up felony charges and jailed in San Luís Potosí under house arrest in the summer of 1910. As a result Madero became ineligible to stand for election and Díaz swept the balloting for a sixth term.

In July 1910 Madero fled from San Luis Potosí to San Antonio, Texas, where he transformed the Anti-reelectionist political organization into a revolutionary apparatus and began planning for revolution to begin on November 20. He relied on political allies that he had recruited personally during his campaign trips. He envisioned a political revolution that would bring democracy to his nation and expressed his goals in the slogans "Effective Suffrage" (that is, honest voting), "No Reelection" (to prevent the Díaz pattern of holding office), and "Municipio Libre" (local control of issues such as taxes). Madero's effort to return and lead troops in Coahuila failed, but by identifying leaders who recruited followers—and financing and arming them—he sparked the revolution into life. Rebels appeared in Chihuahua, Puebla, Morelos, and other places.

The Chihuahua revolutionaries commanded by Pascual Orozco and Pancho Villa scored small but successive victories that revealed a modern army's vulnerability to guerrilla warfare, the provincial hostility to the capital city, and the pent-up anger of rural peoples who had been exploited or ignored by the Porfirian regime. Their small groups gained volunteers from the independent mountain communities, and adventure-seeking recruits from across the state and along both sides of the border. Madero's revolutionary junta in El Paso, Texas, soon attracted a motley group of international volunteers that included Giuseppe Garibaldi, grandson of the Italian hero, veterans of the Boer War and wanted felons. Madero formed them into a foreign legion that he attempted to integrate in his insurrectionary force. These foreigners caused a great deal of friction, and following the Madero era few foreigners found their way into the revolutionary armies.

None of the rebel victories occurred in important cities until the battle of Ciudad Juárez. The rebel victory there gave the rebels a port of entry and a major railhead from which to bring in weapons and provisions from the United States. The Madero victory at Ciudad Juarez in April 1911 encouraged small revolutionary bands to appear across the nation and seemed to foretell an uprising of national proportions. Fear that his regime was crumbling brought Díaz into peace negotiations and in May 1911 he, his family, and most of his cabinet left Mexico for exile in Paris. This first phase of the revolution gave no hint of the ubiquitous violence that soon followed.

The revolution that began in 1910 had a personal character

not seen in other social upheavals. The revolutionaries did not act according to a set of principles, a consciousness of economic relationships, or a commitment to ethnic values. They did not plan to overthrow the government. Rather, they wanted to overthrow Porfirio Díaz and his henchmen and return to the mythical glory days of Benito Juarez. After the rebels drove Díaz out, the Porfirian military officers and old-guard plutocrats remained, though they cared nothing about the man or the administration of Francisco Madero. They waited for the moment when they could remove him and place one of their own in the presidential office. Even the anarchists of Flores Magon referred to Madero as "Díaz the Little." Only Madero's expectant revolutionaries respected their leader, but that too began to fade soon after Madero took office.

Madero expected Mexicans to put down their guns, join political parties, and elect local, state, and national leaders who would legislate reform programs. He never moved beyond the view that the revolution had been purely political and all that was needed was to set aside the fraudulent 1910 presidential voting and hold new democratic elections. As for other reforms, Madero looked to newly elected officials, especially in the state and local governments, to assess the needs of their people and to offer reforms. Madero arranged for an acting president to govern the country until elections could be arranged, so that he himself could be elected president and serve a full four-year term. No one had the slightest doubt that he would win in a landslide, but Madero insisted on following procedures.

Francisco León de la Barra (1863–1939) served as acting president. De la Barra was a man of the Porfiriato by birth (Díaz attended his baptism). Through his family and social ties, de la Barra became one of the foremost diplomats of the time. As Díaz expanded the diplomatic corps in the 1890s, he rewarded the talented de la Barra, who served in Buenos Aires. Transferred in 1904 to Brussels as the minister to the low countries, he distinguished himself as a genial and accomplished diplomat who discreetly kept his private opinions to himself. In 1908 he replaced Enrique Creel as the ambassador in Washington DC, the pinnacle of his career and the only post in the diplomatic service that carried the title of ambassador. Relations between Mexico and the United States had been strained over Chamizal Island in the Rio Grande, over Colorado River water, over the desire of President William Taft to remove the dictator of Nicaragua, and over Japanese interest in a naval base in Baja California. De la Barra's most public success came with arranging the meeting of Taft and Díaz on the Rio Grande border, where the two presidents shook hands in the middle of the international bridge. De la Barra also cultivated close personal relations with Taft and members of his cabinet. He courted Wall Street financiers as honorary president of the New York Mexican Club, whose membership included Andrew Carnegie among other financial giants. He took credit for reviving interest in investing in Mexico, which had tapered off because of the recession of 1907 (although he personally did not invest in Porfirian development). He lived on his government salary and family resources.

From Madero's standpoint de la Barra had all the qualities one needed in an interim president: he could reassure Washington, he had contacts with foreign financiers, he enjoyed the trust of European governments and diplomats, and, perhaps most important, he did not have political ambitions. De la Barra's long service abroad disconnected him from the internal functioning of the Díaz regime, and thus Mexicans did not link him directly to the departed regime. De la Barra appeared to be a neutral bridge between the old government and the pending reformed administration ostensibly based on effective suffrage. In many ways his brief tenure as president (May 26–November 6, 1911) provided a preview of the Madero administration.

The central problem to be solved, de La Barra and Madero believed, was the restoration of social order. Maderista groups, some formed after the Treaty of Juárez that theoretically reestablished peace with Díaz's resignation, wanted a share of the spoils of victory. Many wanted land, but a few wanted whatever they could carry away. Armed bands entered cities and towns, where they sometimes met resistance. In a poor country, sacking villages and small towns offered little, and what could be seized had to be torn from hands as impoverished as those that made up revolutionary armies. The army garrison in Durango for a time fended off some three thousand Maderistas who eventually entered the city to loot and rob its civilian inhabitants. In Cholula a band of self-declared Maderistas burned the archives with land titles and made off with the municipal treasury. Disorder and violence ranged from the annoying to the destructive.

Demobilization of Maderistas seemed prudent. President de la Barra and President-in-waiting Madero understood that only a small percentage of revolutionaries could be incorporated into the federal army or the rural constabulary (called the Rurales). Madero developed a plan to offer the vast majority twenty-five to forty pesos to turn in their weapons and be mustered out of the ranks. He gave no thought to the danger represented by the floating pool of unemployed ex-revolutionaries his program created.

In the state of Morelos, Emiliano Zapata refused to demobilize or disarm his men. He demanded the return of land that villagers claimed they had lost over the years to large landholders. They wanted Madero to redeem the promise to return their lands that they thought he had made. Madero had been misunderstood. Most of the land in question carried legal titles that both President de la Barra and Madero refused to ignore. Rather than seize and distribute land, they favored setting up a commission to investigate, adjudicate and perhaps compensate villagers. Neither man envisioned a massive land redistribution program.

Porfirian bureaucrats and officers who remained in office in Mexico City argued that Zapata's army disrupted life throughout the nearby state of Morelos and that he had to be brought under control. Madero did his best to appease Zapata, while de la Barra lost patience with him. Zapata repeatedly refused to disarm his men and return to civilian activities. De la Barra and Madero failed to understand that they faced villagers who could not be appeased with political reforms, promises, or due process. They refused to recognize land titles that conflicted with the village memory of their land tenure ("from time immemorial"). Whether the villagers exaggerated their losses or not mattered little. Two parallel lines of reality existed that could not be made to converge. Dispatching the federal army to Morelos under Gen. Victoriano Huerta achieved a temporary respite.

Urban labor unrest presented another problem. Many factory owners feared that the revolution might encourage workers to burn down buildings or destroy machinery. President de la Barra understood that workers needed relief and insisted that employers respond to complaints, but he also set legal bounds on strikes. He attempted to act with temperance in response to strikes and demonstrations. In one of his last official acts before the inauguration of Francisco Madero, de la Barra introduced a bill in Congress to establish a labor department in an effort to mediate conflicts in the workplace. De la Barra's brief presidency proved to be the calm before violence engulfed the republic.

As the interim president, de la Barra faced a series of problems that quickly multiplied when Madero took office. Madero assumed control of the existing governmental apparatus that had served the republic under Díaz and that in his view did not need to be replaced. The Porfirian bureaucracy and the federal army remained intact. Madero wanted to share in the political system and open it to more Mexicans, with reforms to limit reelection, provide an honest vote, and restore viable local government. These administrative reforms failed to satisfy many revolutionaries, and revolts broke out against his government from all sides. Unhappy rebels included Emiliano Zapata, who demanded land for villagers in the south, and Pascual Orozco, who insisted on rewards for the revolutionaries. Unreconciled Porfirians, such as Gen. Bernardo Reyes in the north and Gen. Felix Díaz on the east coast, also challenged the regime.

Madero had served for little more than a year when traitorous military officers ordered an attack on the presidential palace. The assault failed because General Reyes, freed from prison, spent over an hour on his personal grooming and the suborned presidential guards changed, so they resorted to an artillery bombardment of the center of town to force Madero from office. Troops for and against Madero battled from February 3 to February 13, 1913, in a battle known as "the Ten Tragic Days." This fighting brought the violence of the revolution to the capital city for the first time. Civilians suffered the greatest number of casualties, reaching the point that corpses had to be burned in the street to prevent the spread of disease. Only when the U.S. ambassador, Henry Lane Wilson, conspired to end the Madero regime by arranging a meeting between opposing commanders did the vicious fighting stop in downtown Mexico City. Gen. Felix Díaz, who commanded the Porfirian military officers opposed to the president, and Gen. Victoriano Huerta, who led the presidential defense, made a treaty of villainy. They agreed to end the fighting, arrest Madero and his vice president, José María Pino Suárez, and establish a new government under military leadership. After less than a week, army guards ostensibly moving the two political prisoners to a safer prison carried out orders to assassinate them. The murders of Madero and Pino Suárez made them revolutionary and national martyrs.

Revolution after Madero

Victoriano Huerta seized the office of president with Madero's imprisonment. The deposed president's assassination on February 22, 1913, ended any political self-restraint. In the capital city, Huerta and Felix Díaz, the nephew of Porfirio, seduced followers with promises of powerful positions in a new Porfirian order. Fear aided recruitment, as army thugs beat up and murdered prominent opposition congressmen and governors. Huerta quickly used troops to establish control in the central states and demanded recognition from governors. It became the season to choose sides.

The news from Mexico City shocked northerners. Deciding whether to align with Huerta or resist him paralyzed Sonora's Governor José María Maytorena, who eventually slipped across the U.S. border. Only three northern governors confronted Huerta, and of these one held office in Sonora as the acting governor. These paltry numbers thinned when federal troops arrested Gov. Abraham Gonzáles of Chihuahua and murdered him by pushing him under a train.

Loyal followers of Madero and others appalled by the army's insurrection and murder of the president joined forces to resist Huerta. In Madero's home state of Coahuila, the governor, Venustiano Carranza, survived to lead the resistance to Huerta. For all Carranza's posturing and preening, he let his own ambitions guide him to become the self-proclaimed "First Chief" and set out to avenge the murdered Madero, topple Huerta, and occupy the presidential chair. The Monoclova Convention (April 1913), signed by various representatives of northern states, gave some legal standing to Carranza's pretensions. Carranza as the First Chief roughly coordinated the northern response to Huerta. He did not command troops, but, like Madero and Benito Juárez before him, he attended to political matters. He wanted to remain a civilian who could occupy the presidency. Order, in the form of constitutional procedures, which provided the name "Constitutionalists" for this military force, appeared vital to the long-term success of the revolution. Carranza made alliances with other powerful northern military leaders, including Álvaro Obregón of Sonora, who proved critical to Carranza's campaign.

The two men came from different classes and experienced life from completely opposing perspectives. Carranza, a Porfirian of the old school, thought much like Madero, while Obregón, informally educated and a farmer by trade, understood the world of manual labor and the obstacles to upward mobility for ambitious individuals of modest means. Well-liked and at ease with people across classes, Obregón had the knack of sizing up people accurately and gaining their confidence and respect. The youngest (born in 1880) of a family of eighteen children, with marriage ties to some better-off families, he had many useful contacts but remained one of the poor relatives. After a series of marginal businesses he acquired a small amount of land to grow garbanzo beans for the export market. He did not participate in the early revolution, but he did become a Maderista.

Obregón's first involvement in politics came with his election as municipal president of his hometown, Huatabampo. In a close, contested election, the winning margin came from Mayo Indian supporters and rural workers. The adolescent Álvaro had many childhood friends among the Mayo Indians and spoke their language. Mayo and Yaqui Indians subsequently proved to be loyal soldiers under his command. As municipal president he applied the community's limited finances to primary schooling and basic improvements, such as access to clean water. Following the coup in Mexico City, Obregón refused to accept Huerta's seizure of power and demanded an armed response. The acting governor, a Maderista, appointed Obregón as head of the state military department. As it turned out, Obregón's background suited the revolutionary generation and its politics of personal trust and sudden betrayal. In contrast, Carranza came from an earlier generation; his approach and policies appeared more suitable for times past and they ultimately failed. Of the two, the Sonoran revolutionary did more to shape revolutionary programs. Obregón represented the new generation that began to emerge as leaders of the revolution.

Obregón hoped to open room for the entrepreneurial middle class. He believed it had been this social group that provided the foundation of the north's transformation from a frontier zone in the early 1870s and 1880s into the fastest-growing region in the republic by 1910. The struggle of his own family for respect and economic gain may have been the mental template he had in mind. Obregón had crossed social boundaries by going from president of a small municipality to a colonel, then to general. Others from Obregon's generation came forward to join the renewed revolution.

Another northerner intent on riding the revolution as far and as high as it would take him was Pancho Villa from Chihuahua. Like Obregón in many ways—young, daring, and eager to make his mark—Villa had joined Madero and then Carranza without lofty or long-range social programs. Personal ambition can too easily be dismissed as a negative characteristic. For saints and martyrs, ambition may be unacceptable, but among revolutionaries it often goes hand in glove with a leader's commitment to achieve a better life for his revolutionary followers. Villa represented his people in the north who had left their villages to work in the mines and larger towns and were set adrift without ties to their home communities. Their hopes crossed back and forth, from land in the countryside to opportunities in town, but always included an anti-foreign tinge in their demands for fair treatment for all Mexicans.

Villa, who had left a career as a bandit to join the revolution, represented the disinherited peoples of society. Like many others dispossessed by the economic policies of the Porfiriato, land and village life dominated his thoughts. Villa's pretensions did not immediately extend to the presidency, but battlefield successes overcame the insecurities that an impoverished youth and criminal livelihood had bequeathed him. For each person who saw him as Robin Hood, another saw him as a predator. Nevertheless, his successes gave him a place in the first rank of the revolution.

The wild card was not a northerner but a revolutionary who occupied a strategic location in Morelos, within striking distance of Mexico City and the important secondary city of Puebla. Emiliano Zapata, the village farmer and horse trainer who had battled against Díaz, Madero, and Huerta, remained constant in his revolutionary demand for land. He and his army of peasants and textile workers had more in common with Villa than with Carranza or Obregón.

As the campaign against Huerta started to unfold, an outside factor of great influence emerged: U.S. president Woodrow Wilson, who demonstrated little self-restraint in his policies toward Mexico. His self-confidence as the organizer of world politics found expression in a comment of his that can be roughly paraphrased, "We'll teach Mexicans to elect good men." Wilson ordered Huerta to hold elections and when he did not receive the immediate assurances that his directions would be carried out, the president moved the considerable influence of the United States to support the Constitutionalists. The United States acted to interdict the sale of war matériel to Huerta and, on the pretext of a foolish insult, occupied the port of Tampico. When some of Huerta's troops mistakenly arrested a U.S. naval patrol in Tampico purchasing oil, Wilson demanded a salute to the U.S. flag as an apology. Huerta refused, unless the United States returned the 21-gun salute—a tacit recognition of the Huerta regime. In response to Huerta, the U.S. Navy occupied the port city. After sending blue jackets into Tampico, Wilson directed the admiral of the fleet to send troops to occupy the main port of Veracruz. Again the U.S. president found a flimsy pretext, claiming that arms and ammunition purchased in the United States (an illegal act because of the embargo in effect against Mexico) had been shipped to Huerta on a German vessel. Wilson concluded that only by occupying the port could the United States impose its self-declared boycott. U.S. marines and sailors landed and occupied the city.

The U.S invasion—the arrogant action that characterized U.S. interventionist policies throughout the Americas in the absence of diplomacy—nearly united Mexicans against the American troops. Across the republic, the aroused sense of nationalism prompted Mexicans to consider a joint campaign against the invaders. Ultimately most settled on Huerta as the more immediate evil and the campaign against him continued. Even in these circumstances, widespread hostility to the United States resurfaced (the nearly genetic combination of hatred and fear that resulted from the U.S.-Mexican War) as students and young people refused to smoke U.S. brands of cigarettes, and rejected U.S. novels and any other form of U.S. culture. United States citizens began fleeing the country, the Veracruz invasion doing what the revolution had not, making them fear for their lives. In the midst of the reaction to Veracruz, few noted the irony that the weapons used as the pretext for the invasion were delivered to Huerta's armies at a port south of Veracruz.

The rank-and-file revolutionaries, many of whom had enlisted in late 1910 and fought against the federal army (1910-1911) and Orozco's insurgents (1912), had become a seasoned and hardened fighting force. The Constitutionalists fused them with new recruits into three armies that reflected the mountainous divisions that ran north to south in parallel lines and the separate manpower pools of each region. Each army developed a different culture and the men formed intense personal loyalty to their commanding general. As a result they could be seen as political factions as much as military units.

The Army of the West under Colonel Obregón occupied locations in Sonora and Sinaloa. In the neighboring state of Chihuahua, General Villa's Division del Norte, the Army of the North, was poised for the march south, while in the eastern border region Pablo Gonzáles commanded the Army of the Northeast. In the south, Carranza pretended that he controlled Zapata's army, referring to it as the Liberating Army of the South. In an indication of trouble to come, the Zapatistas called their force the Liberating Army of the Mexican Nation.

A host of subordinate officers rose to prominence in the shadows of Obregón, Villa, Zapata, and to a lesser extent Gonzáles. For example, Obregón had young commanders, including Benjamín Hill and Salvador Alvarado, who had fought and survived the first revolutionary battles. Other members of his army included the police commissioner of Agua Prieta, Plutarco Elías Calles; the private secretary of the exiled governor, Francisco Serrano;

and the municipal president of the mining town of Cananea, Manuel M. Diéguez. Similar men appeared in the other Constitutionalist armies, and the men who survived often made their mark in the continuous process that spun off new generals and colonels who controlled their own troops. Officers often faced the scarcity of soldiers, and, as a result, offered battlefield prisoners the choice of execution or switching sides. Many served several commanders as the revolution became the common experience of this generation.

The Constitutionalists used the railroads whenever possible to surge southward. Villa's armies had the most success and the most direct route to the capital city. Villa developed his army around his cavalry. He faced large numbers of Federales commanded by professional officers; nevertheless his Dorados, the Golden Ones, appeared unstoppable. Villa's success in central Mexico created a bitter rivalry with Carranza, and the First Chief had no intention of allowing the upstart one-time bandit to reach Mexico City first. He withheld or delayed coal shipments necessary for Villa's locomotives. His choice, Gen. Pablo González in the Northeast, lacked both direct railroad connections south and daring as a commander (he became known as the general who never won a battle). Carranza soon ordered Villa to assist in the capture of Saltillo in the northeast and constantly tried to have him aid Gonzalez. But Villa had a mind of his own and simply ignored telegrams from the First Chief.

Meanwhile, the Constitutionalists Army of the West, led by Gen. Alvaro Obregón, rolled down the coastal railway, capturing Guadalajara and then beginning the southeastern swing toward Mexico City, a section without a railroad connection. This campaign had some unique elements. In a sea battle off the coast of Mazatlán, the Huertista warship *Morelos* sank the revolutionary ship *Tampico*. The Constitutionalists disabled the gunboat *Morelos*, allowing an amphibious landing that succeeded in capturing the island penal colony of Tres Marías from the Federales. No doubt some of the prisoners provided a new group of recruits. A notable sea and air engagement (April 1914) involved the Constitutionalist airplane *Sonora* piloted by Captain Gustavo Salinas dropping bombs on federal warships off the coast of Topolobampo. On another mission Captain Salinas bombed the port of Mazatlán. These engagements represented the world's first use of aircraft in warfare.

Huerta, as his regime collapsed around him, found that even sympathetic international powers refused him aid, so he fled into exile, initially in Spain. His departure only days before Obregón's arrival in the capital city set the stage for the most vicious turn of the revolution. Following the flight of Huerta, the revolutionaries, already divided by bitter rivalries, especially between Carranza and Villa, but including all the major leaders, turned on each other. The lessons of four years of grim, if sporadic, revolution taught that compromise, reconciliation, pardon, and trust served as the weapons of suicide. Execution or exile of obvious enemies, suspicion of everyone except the closest associates, and doubts about even them served as the weapons of survival. These lessons revealed the nature of the revolution.

It had taken sixteen months to defeat Huerta and destroy the federal army. Obregón entered Mexico City in August 1914, paid a symbolic visit to Madero's grave, and began preparations for Carranza's entrance. Obregón paraded at the First Chief's right hand as he accepted the capital from his best general. In nearby Morelos, Zapata received emissaries from both Villa and Carranza. With his own agenda, Villa drifted into opposition to the First Chief whom he dismissively referred to as "the perfumed one," charging that he perfumed his full beard. General Obregón, after some wavering, joined the First Chief, who was anxious to avoid Madero's fate and insisted on the disbandment of the defeated federal army. Federal army general José Rufugio and Obregón signed the Treaty of Teoloyucán, providing for the surrender of weapons, demobilization of all officers and enlisted men, and the turning over of military installations. Ex-Federales had little difficulty finding a revolutionary general to serve.

With Obregón's troops in Mexico City, Zapata's men on its south edge, Villa's army camped at Aguascalientes, and Carranza's forces in San Luis Potosí, an eerie pause occurred. Almost in slow motion, military envoys assembled in Aguascalientes. Villa invited men with military rank only, in a deliberate plan to exclude Carranza. Delegates to the Aguascalientes meeting had to command at least one thousand troops. The convention, again at Villa's behest, considered how to organize victory. Villa and Zapata's representatives ignored Carranza's claims to leadership, and attempted to preempt charges of ambition by choosing neither of their leaders. They selected Gen. Eulalio Gutiérrez, governor of San Luis Potosí, who supported Villa, as provisional president. This represented a political skirmish to establish legitimate control of the capital. Violence, the political currency of the times, quickly reasserted itself.

Carranza's men withdrew as the First Chief refused to recognize the Aguascalientes convention and its president. Zapata and

Villa prepared to impose the convention's presidential choice on the nation. Gutiérrez, of course, had his own army and prepared to use it. Some seventy-two thousand men prepared to occupy the capital. Together they formed the Conventionists. A thoughtful Obregón stepped away from the conflict to assess his course of action. These events moved in a curious calm. For a moment, the peace held. Then Obregón decided to join Carranza, and the Constitutionalists and Conventionists collided in a vicious war between these previous allies. Neither side practiced any form of restraint—because the winner would claim Mexico.

Carranza, faced with a Conventionist army at the gates of the capital, would have been undone had Obregón sided with his fellow generals. Obregón expected to be rewarded at a later date with a presidential term. Carranza withdrew to the safety of Veracruz. Prodded by Obregón, he reluctantly issued some reform decrees designed to bolster his support among the working class. This was part of a deal brokered by Obregón. He had convinced the anarchist workers of the Casa del Obrero Mundial to join him in exchange for some reforms in their favor.

Villa and Zapata occupied the capital and Zapatistas briefly held the nearby city of Puebla. Regrouping his forces, General Obregón forced his way into Mexico City. Violence in a furious kaleidoscope careened across the nation, not everywhere at once and not at the same time, from 1914 to 1920. In frightening and deadly succession, the Constitutionalists and Conventionists killed each other in battles for Mexico City, the cities of the east (the United States played a role here by evacuating Veracruz and leaving a storehouse of armaments to Carranza), at El Ebano, and—the largest and most costly in lives—at Celaya (twice) and Zacatecas. The battle at Celaya in April 1915 tested Villa's cavalry against Obregón's well-armed and well-trained forces. Villa lost 1,800 men in the initial charge. Undeterred he threw wave after wave against Obregón over the course of several days. An estimated twenty-five thousand Villistas failed to overwhelm Obregón's nine thousand defenders. Some six thousand cavalry hidden from Villa made a sudden and decisive attack. Villa lost ten thousand, four thousand killed and another six thousand taken prisoner. Subsequently, Obregón mopping up some Villistas at Trinidad, lost his lower right arm to a sniper bullet.

The grim, wanton violence came not at the major battles fought by leading generals, but in the random shootouts, ambushes, and murders accompanied by the taking of hostages and the sacking of villages. The residents of Tepostlán, Morelos, fled to nearby hiding places in the forest whether it was Zapatistas, Carrancistas, or any other armed band spotted on the road to their town. Allegiance mattered little, because every group foraged horses in the cornfields, and sacked houses for food and anything else they needed, or looted for things someone suddenly wanted. By mid-1915, Carranza's and Obregón's armies had won enough battles (especially at Celaya) to insure that the Convention supporters would never claim the nation, but they had eliminated neither Villa nor Zapata, and violence continued.

The widely dispersed small bands of revolutionaries caused an epidemic of violence that included cruel and patriotic conduct, often by the same person. The violence destroyed day-to-day behavior because of the insecurity it inspired. Individuals fled to the cities or into exile to escape it. Because of the widely dispersed nature of the revolutionary actions, much of it remained outside the record, unknown. Neither newspaper accounts nor memoirs could do more than report part of these small victories and defeats of the insurrectionary movement. In cultural terms, violence made some activities impractical, such as the purchase and use of phonograph players and recorded music, as both proved easy targets for looting—the spring-driven players could be played in rebel camps. The sources that provided immediacy to this upheaval were still photographs, with both the posed and candid images of revolutionaries and the dead, and the popular songs, the *corridos*, which recorded the actions of heroes, villains, and ordinary rebels. With these media, the revolution spawned popular forms of culture.

The failure of printed news and the decline of music recordings reinvigorated the *corrido*. This traditional song reported major events, small tragedies, heroic actions, and wanton brutality, and became a reliable reflection of revolutionary events and the revolutionaries themselves. The cycle of songs, for example, about Villa, his revolution, his men—Los Dorados, and even his horse—Siete Leguas, especially the *corrido* "La Cucaracha," captured his popular character and the public imagination. The recording industry in Mexico City (Columbia, established in 1904, and Victor, in 1905) had focused on waltzes and concert music, and now languished as singers across the countryside reported the revolution in the *corrido* form. In time some *corridos* were recorded; besides those about Villa, the most famous personified the women in the revolution, in "La Adelita."

Because of the song, "Adelitas" served as one name for women who had an active role in the revolutionary campaign. Many fought as *soldaderas*, some even disguised as men to avoid difficulties that might result in battle, especially if taken prisoner. Perhaps the highest-ranking woman in the Constitutionalist forces was Col. Juana Flores, widow of a mine owner. Many more, occasionally with children in tow, served as the commissary for rebel troops, scavenging for food and water, preparing meals, caring for the wounded, and burying their dead.

Still the fighting continued. Zapata and Villa both retreated to their home territories and continued to threaten the new regime created by Carranza and Obregón. Zapata, south of Mexico City, continued to raid haciendas in the region, becoming the personification of the peasantry's demand for land. His actions became the unspoken voice of the country people, at least according to popular mythology. Villa fell back to the North, particularly to Chihuahua. His reputation as the champion of the underdogs received its greatest boost March 6, 1916. Villa, in a brilliant and daring stroke, sent a lightning attack across the international boundary to raid the small U.S. cavalry outpost of Columbus, in New Mexico Territory. Most of the detachment of troopers had left earlier in the day on weekend passes to El Paso, Texas. The raiders struck their primary target, the main hotel and home of the Ravel brothers. The Ravels had run guns for Villa, until his last order when they had decided he had lost the war, so they took the cash and had not delivered the guns. Villa's men learned that the brothers had gone to Albuquerque, so they grabbed the only Ravel around, a young nephew. As the raiders pulled the child down the street, one of the few remaining troopers shot one of the kidnappers and the child then quickly slipped away from his other captor and escaped. The raiders shot up the town, set fire to some buildings, and drove off whatever horses they spotted. Villa's raid on a gringo town electrified all Mexicans with pride, whether or not they supported Villa.

The Columbus raid made Villa a national hero, even among those supporting both Carranza and Obregón, who wanted him out of national politics. The attack demanded action from the United States, but President Woodrow Wilson feared being bogged down in Mexico when he expected his country would soon enter the war in Europe. As a result, he ordered a punitive force after Villa. Mexicans, of course, offered no help to the invaders.

Gen. John J. Pershing, who commanded the punitive expedition, endured a disastrous dress rehearsal for the U.S. entry into world war. The mobilization of both regular and reserve troops, the experiments with mechanized transport (both trucks and airplanes), and the system of command all proved shockingly inept and flawed. All the difficulties revealed in the Spanish-American war had been ignored, not solved. To watching military experts, especially the German high command, the U.S. Army's efforts to organize and execute the punitive expedition seemed farcical. The Germans lost all respect, hence fear, for the U.S. military. The German decision to engage in unrestricted submarine warfare rested in large part on the High Command's conclusions about these weaknesses.

Pershing and his troops, guided by Mormon colonists, and waited on by Chinese cooks and launderers, both groups living south of the border, wandered around Chihuahua for about a year. The expedition never caught Villa, nor his men, and fought only one battle, against Carranza's troops at Parral. Finally, with the European war demanding his attention, Wilson declared the punitive campaign a success and called Pershing home. Unsuccessful from the U.S. perspective, whatever the president stated, the punitive campaign served Carranza well, bottling up one of his major rivals in Chihuahua.

In 1916, with his election to president, Carranza devoted his attention to regularizing his government, pacifying where he could, and convening a constitutional convention in Querétaro. The president did not envision a new and radical constitution, rather he hoped to revise the 1857 document to reflect revolutionary changes. The convention admitted only delegates loyal to Carranza. No unredeemed followers of Villa or Zapata participated. Nevertheless the delegates soon abandoned the president's directions and decided to write a new document. Led by Francisco Mújica from Michoacán, who intensely believed in nationalism and social revolution, the delegates wrote a remarkable statement outlining a national government and a people committed to social justice, economic opportunity, and political participation.

The new constitution of 1917 dictated changes that reflected the goals of different revolutionaries, whether or not they had been Carrancistas. Early opportunistic decrees of Carranza, not meant as statements of enduring principles, were included, much to the president's annoyance. His December 1914 "Addition to the Plan of Guadalupe" and the early 1915 "Law of Restoration and Donation of Ejidos," which had been designed only for the moment, became constitutional objectives to provide land to those who worked it. Mújica persuaded delegates to include sweeping statements on education, labor, agrarian reform, and regulation of the church. Another article took up the fundamental question of land ownership, calling for the return of lands to communities and indigenous groups (for example, the Yaquis and Mayos of Sonora). This clearly expressed a widespread concern of rural, self-sufficient villagers (*labradores*) and highlanders (*serranos*), most clearly personified by Zapata but represented by a cluster of leaders. In another provision, the delegates redeemed Obregón's promise to organized labor through the 'House of World Workers' and gave workers the most advanced statement of rights in the world. In still another article, delegates prohibited monopolies harmful to social interests, implying a guarantee of food and shelter at reasonable prices to the entire population. Finally, two overriding concerns clearly emerged in the document's guarantees for a reasonable life. These were declarations that included restrictions on foreigners and nationalization of all properties of the Roman Catholic Church.

Carranza ignored the document, nevertheless the new constitution of 1917 appealed to Mexicans hoping for substantial change and a new government orientation toward their needs. It mentioned the working class fifty times. Article 27 (land) and article 123 (labor) provided the basis for formative legislation. The idea of economic balance evident in article 28, that directed the government to prevent ruinous industrial competition, provided the foundation for government intervention in all aspects of the economy, including wages, prices and profits, and suggested government-owned industries. Its connection with the liberalism of Benito Juarez was evident in provisions that directed the expropriation of all Catholic Church properties, limited the number of priests (to be determined by each state governor), and stripped away political rights of Church officials. Of great consequence, the principle of social justice trumped private property rights, enabling the federal government to rearrange property in the interest of social justice and national needs.

In response to the constitution, Gov. Gustavo Espinoza Mireles of Coahuila called a labor convention in Saltillo in 1918. The American Federation of Labor (AFL) sent a representative. Craft unions, mainly in the North, joined together to form the Regional Confederation of Mexican Workers (CROM), led by Luis M. Morones, soon to become the most powerful labor leader in the republic. Contributing to the false sense that the nation had turned away from an unpredictable plunge into violence, the Zapatista stronghold of the state of Morelos had been pacified. In an outrageous subterfuge, Col. Jesús M. Guajardo succeeded in assassinating Zapata and snuffing out his rebellion. In 1919 Guajardo received promotion to general, along with fifty thousand pesos. Zapata's murder notwithstanding, the optimistic dared to believe that revolutionary violence had run its course.

It had not. In 1920, the decade ended as it had began—with violence, provoked by a presidential election. Neither Díaz in 1910, nor Carranza in 1920 allowed voters a free hand. Díaz chose to impose himself; Carranza attempted to impose Ignacio Bonillas, a civilian who had served the president in Washington in a number of capacities before becoming the ambassador to the United States, and appeared to be a compliant successor. Bonillas, originally from Sonora and married to a U.S. woman, had missed the violence of the early revolution. Opponents considered him to be *agringado* (Americanized) and referred to him as "Mr. Bonillas." It is debatable whether or not any revolutionary general would have passively accepted the Bonillas imposition.

Carranza's chief of military operation in several states, Pablo González, refused to support Bonillas and subsequently announced his own candidacy, but eventually withdrew rather than face Obregón. Nevertheless, Bonillas appealed to the civilian upper and middle class, anxious to move beyond the confusion and violence they associated with revolutionary generals. In reality the revolution had not played itself out to the point that *civilismo* had any chance of success.

Obregón, confident that he would be selected, had resigned as minister of war and returned to Sonora to await the summons to presidential duty—but it never came. Finally, he could wait no more and proclaimed his candidacy for the presidential office, informing Carranza by telegraph. Obregón's proclamation accused Carranza of corruption in office and indifference to the social needs of the nation. In fact, most of it could not be denied. The president had allowed his subordinates to enrich themselves and had not hesitated to take his share. Obregón campaigned widely, held conversations with governors and generals, and gave impassioned speeches in spite of obstructionism and intimidation by Carranza agents and police. It seemed only a question of time before the break between the two would become more serious.

Bad faith, betrayal, and violence joined the campaign. Obregón, ordered by the minister of war to appear in Mexico City to testify in a court-martial, decided against all advice to go. It became obvious that Carranza intended to implicate Obregón in a plot as a pretext to imprison him. A wary Obregón stayed with high-profile old friends and socialized with them, including Gen. Benjamin Hill, commander of military forces in the capital. Summoned once again to testify, he did not respond. He fled the city: a driver took him through town, and he jumped from the moving car as it passed through a park, and then went to railroad yards. With the help of rail workers and disguised as a railroad man—complete with a lantern and a coat hanging off his right shoulder to hide his missing lower arm, he left the city on a train to Iguala. Within hours of his escape the police came to arrest him. Subsequently, Carranza telegraphed all governors and military regional commanders to arrest Obregón on sight.

Rebellion remained General Obregón's only option. Joining with Plutarco Calles and Adolfo de la Huerta, Obregón constituted the Sonora Triangle and formulated the Plan of Agua Prieta. Their statement declared that Carranza had forfeited his legitimacy and ceased to be the constitutional president. Within hours, telegrams poured in, pledging support to Obregón in his struggle against the Carranza regime. Generals and colonels, many who began their careers under Obregón (including General Hill), deserted the government. Mexico City fell easily into Obregón's remaining hand.

Almost too late, Carranza set out for Veracruz with the idea of establishing a temporary capital. Veracruz under the control of Gen. Guadalupe Sánchez, at the time still loyal to Carranza, seemed secure. Carranza left Mexico City by rail. Several trains, including the presidential Golden Train, stretched over eight miles. Some eight to ten thousand people crowded aboard, along with the approximately eight million in gold pesos, mint equipment, government papers, and a variety of military equipment and horses. Carranza just made it. The trains bringing up the rear were captured, but at least half the trains escaped, pulling away from a pursuing locomotive. But Carranza's luck did not hold. General Sánchez switched sides, dooming the plans for a temporary capital in the port city. Then the lead train encountered a section of destroyed track, and water for the locomotive boilers could not be found. Meanwhile, several attacks had to be repulsed. Carranza left the train and with a mounted escort headed north, vowing to fight to the end. He managed to cross the mountains into northern Puebla where he planned to spend the night in a modest hut in Tlaxcalontongo. At four in the morning, attackers killed the sleeping president as he lay on the dirt floor. His assassins stripped the bleeding corpse of glasses, watch, items of clothing, and other things they coveted. As President Carranza had predicted as he fled the capital, now the people would see "how a president of the Republic dies." Obregón ordered an investigation of Carranza's murder, but no one was ever arrested or punished.

The Sonora Triangle overthrew Carranza and created the conditions that led to his murder. Alvaro Obregón, Plutarco Calles, and Adolfo de la Huerta, all from the same state, took power in 1920. The Sonora dynasty dominated the nation until 1936. These three men inaugurated a more constructive phase of the revolution, attempting to implement the provisions of the 1917 constitution that framed social change. They promoted general education, organized labor, and agrarian reform. Their anti-church policies and bitter politics also provoked widespread violence, at times bordering on gangsterism.

Continuity in the Midst of Revolution

Mexicans have a strong attachment to constitutional forms, although everyone recognized then that actions often fell far short of their spirit and intent. The continuity of the government's bureaucracy provided a stable political stratum that functioned beneath the level of chaos dominated by revolutionary generals and their armies. The presidents of the Sonora Triangle were committed to the constitution of 1917 and used their plans to implement it to obtain legitimacy, rally public support, and administer the republic.

The revolution as Madero had first defined it insisted on democratic elections for the constitutional president of the republic. Congress and Obregón (just as Madero earlier suggested, a provisional president), named Adolfo de la Huerta president for the six-month term necessary to arrange elections. Carranza, Obregón, Calles, and the later revolutionary presidents maintained constitutional forms at the same time that they clarified votes as they believed necessary.

The federal legislature and the bureaucracy remained as institutional islands in a sea of violent uncertainty. Nevertheless it should be noted that occasionally shootings took place in the halls of Congress, as most of the representatives carried guns to sessions. Armies directed as personal political factions attempted to destroy each other, but not the constitutional framework of the republic. The traditional patriotic myths and rituals continued to receive attention. Although Benito Juarez, traditional liberalism, and the constitution of 1857 formed the icons of the past, they still provided the restorative spiritual ideals of the nation. Revolutionary contenders for the presidential prize understood that they needed to be constitutional leaders. Constitutionality conveyed legitimacy that the battlefield could not, even for the most distinguished revolutionary generals.

The bureaucratic activity juxtaposed revolutionary violence

and provided continuity to the programs that had been implemented initially during the Porfiriato. Conservation of natural resources, while of vital importance today, had less urgency in the nineteenth century. The first efforts to control the destruction of forests began under Díaz and continued through the government of President Cardenas, directed by a Porfirian scientist and teacher. Miguel Angel de Quevedo, the aptly nicknamed "Apostle of the Tree," was born into a well-to-do family in 1862, in Guadalajara, and grew up in France. He earned a science degree in 1883 from the University of Bordeaux, and studied at the Ecole Polytechnique in Paris. He studied hydraulic engineering and had become a conservationist by the time he received his degree in 1887. On returning to Mexico he worked on a massive drainage project designed to end flooding in the Valley of Mexico, a project that was finally finished in 1900. Subsequently he served as the director of works at the port of Veracruz. From the former project, he became aware of the impact of deforestation. Dust storms that swept the capital following the draining of the lakes presented a new problem addressed by the Junta Central de Bosques (Forest Committee) created in 1904. Quevedo established a tree nursery in Coyoacán that by 1914 nurtured 2.4 million trees in an effort to reverse the process.

President Madero had supported tree farming, and had put forward a plan to drain swamps and created a forest reserve in Quintana Roo. President de la Huerta's plans for conservation amounted to transplanting trees from the city to his ranch. Nevertheless, between 1913 and 1914 (during the Ten Tragic Days, and the overthrow of Madero), one hundred forty thousand newly planted trees dotted hillsides and dry lakebeds as well as adorned the capital. Once Quevedo returned from exile, he convinced President Carranza to establish the Desierto de los Leones as the first national park and then persuaded the framers of the constitution of 1917 to include conservation language in the document. Subsequently President Cárdenas, an admirer of Quevedo, created forest reserves, protected zones, and more national parks. A number of village lands granted by Cardenas, called *ejidos*, depended on sustainable forest products. While issues such as conservation remained a secondary priority, the point remains that in the midst of battles, conspiracies, assassinations, massacres, flights into exile, and the movement of armies, they were dealt with in a reasonably normal fashion. The bureaucracies remained in place and continued to function. The republic the revolutionaries fought over remained a constitutional and legal one.

As the era of major pitched battles and ubiquitous bloodshed ended, to be followed by a continuation of violence on a small scale and a turn to assassinations, the collective memory of the times came from the wide circulation of photographs of the fighting and especially the dead. Photographers, both those who had produced images for tourists during the late Porfiriato and early photojournalists who came to record the revolution, produced thousands of pictures, many of which became postcards offered for sale. Combined with the *corridos* these photos told the story of the revolution in images and music, with a graphic immediacy unequaled by other media for the general audience. For some, especially foreigners, the photos provided a glimpse of the revolution as an exotic experience; for others, especially nationals, they demonstrated the human cost of what they had begun, and that it was the young from across the nation who were achieving its victories, to create a new regime and new society.

The murder of Carranza severed the last tie to the old regime. He had been a Porfirian bureaucrat turned revolutionary. Now the revolution's leaders all came from the younger generation that would dominate the country through 1946. Still young, they were experienced veterans of revolutionary battles and survivors of its violence. They intended to reshape their country.

Suggested Reading

Cumberland, Charles C. *Mexican Revolution: The Constitutionalist Years*. Austin: University of Texas Press, 1972.

Hart, John M. *Revolutionary Mexico—The Coming and Process of the Mexican Revolution*. Berkeley: University of California Press, 1997.

Katz, Friedrich. *The Life and Times of Pancho Villa*. Stanford CA: Stanford University Press, 1998.

Knight, Alan. *The Mexican Revolution,* 2 volumes. Lincoln: University of Nebraska Press, 1986.

Womack, John. *Zapata and the Mexican Revolution.* New York: Alfred A. Knopf, 1970.

2

THE NEW GENERATION AND REVOLUTION CHANGE

(*Previous page*) 2. Calavera of a flapper. Even common board games included images of emerging social groups like this *calavera* of the new woman of the 1920s and 1930s. From the Champion Mexican Art Collection, Tucson, Arizona. Photograph by Cheryle Champion.

President Alvaro Obregón

Alvaro Obregón, the victorious leader of the Sonora Triangle, selected Sonora civilian Adolfo de la Huerta as the provisional president for the required six-month term, in order to organize an election that Obregón anticipated winning. The new provisional president seemed a good choice. From a banking family respected across the class structure of Sonora, with good relations with the Yaquis and Mayos and service in the state legislature behind him, de la Huerta had all the right contacts. Experience in the United States as the consul general in New York also proved useful. His personal qualities of easy informality and dislike of ceremony fitted the times. Endowed with an excellent voice, he enjoyed singing, accompanied by dramatic flourishes that enchanted his listeners. Gossips reported that he had hoped to sing with the New York Metropolitan Opera. De la Huerta represented the quintessential civilian, in keeping with Obregón's desire to dilute untrustworthy generals with competent nonmilitary professionals.

Just as Francisco de la Barra during his stint as provisional president, de la Huerta permitted time for decompression before the next storm. He handled some tricky issues, often in ways that the less generous found hard to accept. The lingering problem of Pancho Villa still able to disrupt order in Chihuahua but not strong enough to threaten the federal government had to be resolved. Villa indicated that he might retire under the right conditions. Both Obregón and the minister of war, General Calles, preferred him dead, believing that he could not be trusted to stay in retirement and out of trouble. In his agreement with de la Huerta, Villa specified that he could select fifty armed retainers paid by the government. The government also gave him title to a hacienda just across the Chihuahua state line in Durango to keep him occupied with agriculture. The rest of Villa's force of some seven hundred men received a year's pay and title to a plot of land or they were integrated into the army. The written agreement, signed on July 28, 1920, appeared to end Villa's active involvement in politics and was intended to spare him the fate of assassins' bullets suffered by Zapata.

The provisional president also negotiated the retirement of two other opposition generals. Gen. Felix Díaz received more than magnanimous treatment after surrendering in Veracruz. President de la Huerta allowed him to go into exile in Europe in spite of Calles's call for a court-martial, something that likely would have ordered his execution. Pablo Gonzáles, popularly charged as the man who arranged for Col. Jesús M. Guajardo to assassinate Zapata, had been in an abortive rebellion in Monterrey and he also escaped the ultimate penalty. Once de la Huerta ordered his release, González fled across the border into the United States. The interim president replaced vengeance with generosity and his actions displeased those anxious to settle scores. The contrast between the generals who preferred a quick, permanent solution with bullets and the provisional president could not be missed.

President de la Huerta's obvious fairness encouraged holdout

Zapatista generals to reach accommodation with the government. Belligerent Gen. Alberto Pineda O., holding out in Chiapas, yielded to the president's generosity in a similar fashion. When necessary, firmness followed by forgiveness would be used. Col. Esteban Cantú, who controlled Baja California, insisted on supporting Carranza in spite of Carranza's death. Consequently the state became a haven for an assortment of mischief makers. Because it bordered the United States, the potential always existed for serious conflict with Washington. De la Huerta dispatched emissaries to the United States to explain the situation and rally support. He also enlisted the help of various defeated factions, Villista and Huerta sympathizers. As a result Cantú found it difficult to buy arms. A federal expedition added a touch of intimidation and—coupled with negotiations—headed off violence. Cantú prudently left for Los Angeles, California.

President de la Huerta called for all to recognize their common interests, as he attempted to reunite citizens through appeals to nationalism and campaigns for revolutionary programs. De la Huerta's pacification worked, not just because of his personality, but also because all knew that he would serve only a short term as an interim president and that he did not have command of the real currency of the times—revolutionary soldiers. He had quickly begun to arrange for the presidential election.

Obregón faced no serious opposition in the presidential contest. Only one candidate opposed the general, Alfredo Robles Domínguez—put forward by the Partido Nacional Republicano and the Partido Católico—and he had little chance of attracting many voters. Obregón allowed his staff to attack his opponent, making charges, sometimes unfairly, that undermined his creditability. Obregón's travels throughout the country made it clear that he wanted a national consensus behind him. He got it. The results gave Obregón 1,131,751 votes to his opponent's 47,441.

On midnight on November 30, 1920, the president-elect took the oath of office in the chamber of deputies. The new president faced difficult issues and interconnected problems that had to be confronted almost immediately or risk the resumption of violence. Obregón believed that everything hinged on agrarian reform. What happened in the countryside influenced the size of the floating pool of soldiers and the ability of their leaders to threaten order. Moreover the recovery of the economy, needed revenue from taxes, and recognition of the government by foreign nations who served as the source of markets and loans, all could be damaged by the redistribution of property. Obregón cautioned that it would be fatal to dismember the great estates before smaller holdings became viable. He understood that time to resolve the issue remained short. The Law of Ejidos of 1921 provided for communal holdings, setting up village committees to interact with the National Agrarian Commission established by Carranza. In order to make procedures work better, the administration replaced the Law of Ejidos with the Agrarian Regulatory Law of 1922. The new procedure set up steps in four-month segments, at different levels of government, that might finally reach the secretary of agrarian reform for a provisional grant and eventually, with the president's signature, give the *ejido* community permanent title.

The 1922 law made it possible to test whether the villagers or the landowners had the most power and consequently tip the decision in favor of the stronger. But an award of land or a reaffirmation of ownership both implied obligation to the president and the government. Landholders who suffered expropriation received long-term bonds carrying modest interest. Foreigners often refused to accept bonds and appealed to their own governments, but most expropriations involved Mexican owners. Expropriation of commercial agricultural land had an impact on production. The new village owners could not be expected to maintain the same level of export productivity, understandably turning to subsistence crops, while cutting back on commercial production. Land distributed to *ejidos* combined bottomland with rocky hillsides, an overall improvement in a village's prospects but not a total economic transformation. From an economic standpoint it made little sense but from a revolutionary political commitment to social improvement it became necessary.

Obregón distributed some 1,200,000 hectares of land but critics charged that he moved slowly because of the impact on revenues. Public attention focused on the great estates that seemed to personify the old regime's skewed distribution of property. In Chihuahua, Luis Terrazas held 2.5 million hectares of land, the largest single holding in the republic; he and his family owned most of the best land in the state, along with adequate access to water. In good times, they grazed four hundred thousand head of cattle, one hundred thousand sheep, and twenty-four thousand horses. The cattle boom in the 1890s solidified the family's fortune and allowed diversification into manufacturing and banking. Politically the Terrazas properties had to be expropriated, and Obregón did just that.

The Terrazas family had fled the country following Madero's

victory in 1911. In the early revolutionary days Luis fled to El Paso, along with some five million pesos, and subsequently established a bank in Los Angeles, California. He returned to Chihuahua in 1920, after extensive negotiation concluded with the Obregón regime. The government offered thirteen million pesos in compensation, which came in the form of assets transferred from the Caja de Prestamos para Obras de Irrigation y Fomento de Agricultura (the agricultural irrigation and development loan office). Obregón made it clear that he wanted Luis and his family to resume their entrepreneurial activities. Terrazas's son-in-law Enrique Creel also returned to open a Mexico City bank and become an advisor to President Obregón. The family network of international investors and financiers served the country well, although mostly behind the scenes.

As government officials dealt with issues of land reform, they also faced international difficulties. Formal recognition of the government became a pressing problem. For a chronically strapped government, access to financial markets became a crucial objective, but one that depended on international recognition. The chronic violence that began in 1910 led to damage claims by foreign nationals against the Mexican government for injuries, deaths, and loss of property. European countries and the United States demanded settlements or at the least an indication of how claims would be handled before extending diplomatic recognition. Without funds to compensate claimants, the revolutionaries seemed caught in an impossible situation. Moreover, Great Britain, having emerged from World War I virtually bankrupt, hesitated to recognize the Obregón government before the United States did so.

President Obregón unexpectedly faced an economic contraction in 1921. The collapse of commodity prices threatened tax revenues and foreign exchange reserves. Copper, lead, and silver prices fell to ruinous levels, leading to mine closures and unemployed miners. Silver exports dropped almost forty-four million pesos from the previous year. Exports of cattle fell over two-thirds and other commodities experienced a similar price decline. To make matters worse, Mexican workers attracted to the United States by wartime wages, and now suddenly unemployed, became stranded. The government spent almost a million dollars to repatriate them and find them some sort of employment at home to avoid a further catastrophe.

The long-planned establishment of a federal ministry of public education provided a respite from contingency problems. The ministry originally had been planned during the presidency of de la Huerta. José Vasconcelos, rector of the National University, supported the idea and planned the organizational structure of the new ministry well before its formal creation in July 1921. Consequently he seemed the obvious choice to head the new ministry. He based his plan on the ideas developed in the Soviet Union by Anatoly Lunacharsky that called for a tripartite division: schools to teach science and technical education, libraries to offer books and adult classes, and a department to promote the fine arts. The ministry opened federal schools throughout the country in a separate system from the existing state-funded schools. Rafael Ramírez directed new cultural missions, teachers who acted as missionaries in the countryside. Approximately one thousand rural schools opened, many of them quite modest but serviceable. Villagers often built the schools and had a role in what they taught as well as in the selection of teachers. As workshops of revolution, schools adapted to local realities, but most taught Spanish to Indians and fostered a sense of cultural inclusion in the nation. Teachers also had public health responsibilities, instructing adults and children in good hygiene and nutrition.

In addition, Vasconcelos established libraries in the capital. Acquiring printing machinery allowed the ministry to provide cheap copies of the classics and free editions of primary readers to teach the largely illiterate rural inhabitants. Obregón, who had been taught to read by his older siblings, had mixed feelings about distributing Plato and other classics. Nevertheless, he allowed Vasconcelos to indulge grandiose schemes, knowing that if Congress disapproved, the money would not be budgeted. A high point came with the opening of the National Sports Stadium, with some sixty thousand attendees, people in regional dress, and a chorus of twelve thousand children. Vasconcelos demonstrated the strong connection between education and nationalism, a lesson that would not be forgotten.

Petroleum, the one economic bright spot, kept the country afloat. Mexico produced twenty-six percent of the world supply, and demand remained strong as the world moved away from coal. In September 1921, 17,300,000 barrels—a record volume—entered the world market. Fiscal authorities in early June decreed a special export tax that was resisted by the industry. When the government declined to rescind the order, British and American oil interests shut down operations in protest. The matter would be resolved, but the dispute made the point that Mexico could not force large oil companies to conform to regulations. The USS

Sacramento, cruising off the oil fields of Tampico, underscored the reality that the nation had not succeeded in establishing a balance between international pressure and national sovereignty.

President Obregón mounted a propaganda campaign in the United States to portray himself as a businessman. The fact that he grew garbanzo beans on his property in Sonora and exported them to the United States, coupled with the northern Mexican ethos of hard work and entrepreneurship, gave some credence to this image—a businessman who happened to be a general and now president. While it might be difficult to lay aside Obregón's military image, he appeared to consider himself a civilian forced to take up arms in defense of middle-class values and he suggested that recognition by Washington would be sensible for sound business reasons. Groups of U.S. citizens received invitations to come see for themselves that the country had not disappeared amid revolutionary violence. Like Porfirio Díaz before him, Obregón easily socialized with visitors, creating an effective lobby in favor of recognition of his government. The Ministry of Foreign Affairs reportedly spent two million dollars to convince the U.S. general public.

The establishment in 1921 of the Summer School for Foreigners within the National University, based on a Spanish model, appeared to be an attempt to seduce teachers and intellectuals into supporting the revolution at the same time Mexico benefited from their expertise. The school offered inexpensive courses in Spanish language and literature, folklore, archaeology, and Mexican history, taught by distinguished Mexican and foreign scholars. Its twenty-six-week courses aimed at creating understanding and sympatric ties between the Mexico and the United

States. The faculty included such world-renowned intellectuals as John Dewey. Nevertheless, the U.S. consul general in Mexico City, Claude Dawson, reported that the Summer School functioned under the direction of radicals in the Secretariat of Education, implying a more sinister objective.

U.S. government officials worried that Mexicans verged on following the Bolshevik example. Article 27 of the Constitution of 1917 appeared to threaten private property rights and U.S. investments in mining and agriculture. An almost hysterical reaction built up, as influential individuals implied that Obregón intended to do away with private property, the alleged cornerstone of U.S. democracy. Even more alarming was the possibility that radicalism, once established, would spread to other nations in a hemisphere-wide pandemic. U.S. businessmen, especially bankers and oil producers, demanded that the government intervene, as it had in Central America and the Caribbean, to stop the radical contagion. Informal reassurance that the government had no intention of massive assault on property rights or retroactive enforcement of Article 27 failed to reassure officials in Washington. The United States wanted a treaty of friendship and commerce signed before it would recognize the Obregón government. The issues of concern inevitably covered virtually every fear and possibility of the U.S. business community. The Mexican Supreme Court offered a way out of the box that the United States had climbed into over the issue of recognition. The court declared that the provisions of the constitution did not apply retroactively to landowning companies that had made known their intention to extract crude oil.

The court's decision appeared to protect petroleum investments but the issue of commercial landholdings remained. Nevertheless it provided an opening for both sides. The Bucareli Conference in Mexico City began on May 14 and continued until August 15, 1923. The conference allowed both sides to vent their fears and sense of outrage, while talking past each other. At one point the U.S. representatives walked out. An alarmed Obregón called on de la Huerta to save the day. When the conference resumed, the atmosphere had changed. The death of President Harding during the long conference may have underlined how long the issue had dragged on. The U.S. secretary of state, Charles Evans Hughes, after reading the minutes and the closing declarations of both sides, advised his Mexican counterpart that President Coolidge approved and would announce formal recognition. The timing would be adjusted to allow Obregón to report it in his address to Congress on September 1, 1923. The fact that the conference declarations and the minutes served as a formal agreement allowed both sides to interpret matters as they wished. It would not be the end of conflict over the application of the constitution, but the Bucareli Conference had at least regularized relations between the two neighbors.

A large part of Obregón's success externally as well as domestically came from his sense of the possible and willingness to accept it. He understood that containing the ambitions of the generals would not be easy. His strategy had several major components, but it boiled down to forcing many of them into retirement on half salary. He shot some generals, as he said, with a cannonball of fifty thousand pesos, an amount much less than sending the army to bring them to heel, while he made others military zone commanders. Obregón rotated zone commanders frequently, to discourage their developing personal bonds with the troops, and said nothing about pocketing money allocated for other purposes. A handful of the most powerful generals could not be touched and they created personal fiefdoms in various states. None of them had the desire to test Obregón on the battlefield, nor did the president want to plunge into violence to prove his prowess.

Obregón's realism allowed for revolutionary imperatives to be adapted to a particular region. Consequently the revolution viewed from above appeared to be a patchwork of programs, in some cases radical, in others minimal, and in some areas nonexistent. These constituted the many workshops of the revolution that collectively made it function. Obregón favored young university-trained technocrats, not for high political positions, but for planning and bureaucratic effectiveness. He also encouraged the return of the Porfirian elite, along with their skills and their money from El Paso, San Antonio, Los Angeles, New York, and Paris.

The returning exiles found it unwise to be too prominent in society or to take high-profile political positions. Those engaged in nonagricultural enterprises recovered their economic and social positions faster. In the industrial city of Monterrey the elite had limited investments in land. They understood that claims on factories could not be advanced by the dispossessed, although they had to pay attention to new labor codes and their workers to avoid problems. In addition, their contributions aided economic stability and tax revenues. Reintegration into society began with charitable networks established by their wives. The Mexican Red Cross provided useful services in a nonreligious manner to a wide segment of society. Intermarriage with the new revolutionary elite provided regional access to political power for the new generation. At times attempts to make a suitable match among the new elite presented some unpleasant moments, as opportunism clashed with elite culture and values, with little room for romantic love. Nevertheless the merging of elites succeeded in most instances. A typical example of this outcome, the Samaniegos of Cuidad Juarez and El Paso, Texas, regained their wealth and political authority on both sides of the border.

The Sonora Triangle Consolidates Its Hold

Obregón established an uneasy balance between rural Mexico's land hunger and the need to generate revenues from commercial agriculture. Mining posed fewer problems, in spite of revisions of the Porfirian mining laws. The old 1884 mining code allowed ownership provided that the mines remained continuously active—a provision that did not differ that much from ownership remaining with the government while the right to work deposits was in the hands of a company. Miners' complaints could be addressed without raising property issues. Urban workers in a similar fashion could not assert proprietary claims to factories, but could demand changes in working conditions, hours, and wages. Almost all of the issues handled by Obregón could have been introduced during the Porfirato, particularly in the last decade of the nineteenth century, when most of them had been pointed out by Francisco Bulnes, Andrés Molina Enríquez, Wistano Luis Orozco, and others. Radical critiques by the Western Federation of Miners, the Industrial Workers of the World (IWW), Ricardo Flores Magón, and John Kenneth Turner, the American author of *Barbarous Mexico*, among others, might be dismissed, but provided a strong early warning of impending social turmoil.

President Obregón, aware of the intricate but fragile balance that he had succeeded in establishing, preferred to remain in power, but he understood that his reelection could not be imposed on the country without setting off another round of violence. The best alternative appeared to be designating a loyal subordinate as the candidate for the presidency. He turned to those he trusted to share his vision and continue his successful approach. Of the two possibilities—Adolfo de la Huerta and Gen. Plutarco Calles, both Sonorans—Obregón choose the military man rather than the civilian and former interim president. He reasoned that the generals would tolerate only their own. De la Huerta initially supported the choice of Calles. A number of important labor groups, including the Confederación General de Trabajadores, expressed unenthusiastic acceptance of Calles.

Pancho Villa, not a friend of Calles, indicated that he favored de la Huerta and would consider taking to the battlefield if his old friend needed him. His offer to return to battle was taken seriously by members of the Obregón administration. Jesús Salas Barraza, a Durango legislator, saw to it that several killers who had a grievance against Villa received arms, including a machine gun. Salas Barraza reportedly assured the assassins that they would not be punished, implying that a higher authority would protect them. On July 20, 1923, Villa, riding in the front seat of his Dodge, on the way home from an assignation, passed by a rented house in Parral and gunfire riddled his car and body. Salas Barraza took responsibility, although he had not been present in the house. He wrote a confession that was given to President

Obregón. Apprehended on the way to the border, he ended up in the penitentiary in Mexico City, sentenced to twenty-one years. Subsequently transferred to the Parral jail, then the penitentiary in Chihuahua, his release was arranged by Obregón later in the year. Suspicion that Calles had ordered the murder became common throughout the country, but remained supposition until historian Friedrich Katz reconstructed the documents, providing a chain of evidence against Calles. Villa's assassination competed with the news of the Bucareli Conference and the subsequent renewal of diplomatic relations with the United States.

Both Obregón and Calles understood the utility of political parties in the development of a public consensus but they became aware that party politics could not be easily controlled. An explosion of parties had come with the revolution, and none survived. A host of parties—the Laborista, Agrarista, Socialista del Sureste, and others—sought influence and alliances. Congress functioned as an effective counterbalance to the executive branch of government at the time and party bosses had to be reckoned with by the president. While Obregón repeatedly declared that he governed in the interest of the nation, not in the interest of any party, the situation remained more complex until the creation of an official party in 1929.

General Calles counted on several parties to back his presidency bid, but the presidential race at first became entwined with the race for governor of San Luis Potosí. There political confusion resulted in two separate state administrations. Both Obregón and Calles wanted to stay clear of an impossible situation. Meanwhile several prominent generals began to express the view that the army preferred Adolfo de la Huerta over Calles.

Eventually Obregón ordered new elections in San Luis Potosí to resolve the state crisis.

A series of events led de la Huerta to resign as finance minister and declare his candidacy. Bitter charges flew back and forth between the candidates, including allegations that de la Huerta had mismanaged finances to the extent that the president had needed to order pay cuts. In response, the other side claimed that the federal government had damaged the nation in favor of the oil companies by not making Article 27 retroactive. Popular ambivalence turned the straightforward campaign for a successor into a political mess—providing a bitter lesson for both Obregón and Calles.

The breaking up of the Sonora Triangle emboldened other generals envious of Calles's rapid move to the top. Disgruntled Gen. Enrique Estrada began plotting as early as 1922. Gen. Joaquín Amaro informed President Obregón of Estrada's activities, but the president chose not to take it seriously at the time. Ambivalence over Calles and support for de la Huerta required taking military threats much more seriously, as civilian politicians attempted to sway opposition generals. Candidate de la Huerta did not favor an uprising. As the political situation deteriorated, de la Huerta fled to Veracruz where Gen. Guadalupe Sánchez and other officers pressed him to issue the Plan of Veracruz on December 7, 1923, and to assume the title of the Supreme Chief of the Revolution. The plan accused Obregón of destroying the independence of Congress and the Supreme Court and setting things in place to resume the presidency after Calles's term, among other charges. A total of 102 generals joined de la Huerta in revolt.

The rebellion resulted in a wave of assassination that thinned out congressmen who opposed Obregón and Calles, while intimidating the others. Obregón, who took charge of putting down the rebellion, had the advantage of diplomatic recognition, enabling him to buy weapons and ammunitions in the United States, including De Haviland airplanes used for transport and bombing runs. Some 60 percent of the army declared for him. The revolt continued over a three-month period and at least seven thousand soldiers died. Gen. Lázaro Cárdenas, wounded and captured by Estrada, survived to have an expanded role in national politics. Once Obregón defeated the rebellionm, Adolfo de la Huerta fled across the border and ended up in Los Angeles, where he taught voice and violin. In 1936 President Lázaro Cárdenas would appoint him visitor of Mexican consulates, ending his exile. The mild-mannered, soft-spoken de la Huerta had reignited revolutionary violence.

President Plutarco Calles

The inauguration on November 30, 1924, had a celebratory aspect. The ceremony in the new National Stadium before a crowd of thirty thousand—including Samuel Gompers of the AFL and other guests from the United States—suggested a broad political consensus, with congressmen and military men both in attendance. Receiving the presidential sash before such a multitude emphasized the transfer of legitimate power to a constitutional president. The new cabinet included an old acquaintance of Gompers, Luis N. Morones, leader of the Confederación Regional Obrera Mexicana (CROM), appointed minister of industry, commerce, and labor. An intimate of President Calles, avoided by some as a crude, uncultured person, he became the most powerful person after the president. Calles and Morones played poker together at the Sonora-Sinaloa Club, entertained each other at lavish parties, and both had plans for organized labor. Calles envisioned a corporate structure with labor part of the underpinnings of the government and under firm control. Morones used his official position to build union membership to nearly two million under the CROM umbrella. Wages increased and working hours fell to a reasonable eight-hour day. The number of strikes also fell dramatically. In 1924 some 23,988 workers went on strike but that figure dropped by more than half the next year and another 50 percent in 1926. In 1927 there were just seven strikes involving less than five hundred strikers.

During the Calles years, the representatives from the Ministry of Public Health and a variety of voluntary organizations pushed forward anti-alcohol campaigns. The programs, at times favoring temperance and at others prohibition of alcoholic beverages, had roots in the Porfirian years, but had become increasingly important beginning in the Obregón presidency, most often at the community level. The national programs focused on educating the public about the evils of drinking alcohol, through school initiatives, parades, posters, and public forums. The greatest success of the anti-alcoholic efforts, which seemed like racist attacks on indigenous peoples and classist campaigns against the poor, came through the association of temperance with public health. The campaign generally had success only in selected communities, although it certainly created a much greater national awareness of the issues of drunkenness and its relationship to the modern family that the revolutionaries hoped to foster.[1]

Relations with the clergy proved much more difficult than labor relations. Antagonism had deep roots—in mid-nineteenth-century liberalism and the Constitution of 1857, and more recently in the anticlerical articles of the Constitution of 1917. When he took control of Mexico City 1915, General Obregón knew that some clergy had raised money for Victoriano Huerta and the general hounded them to contribute the same amount to the Constitutionalists. Subsequently occasional violent incidents kept resentment high among the faithful. In 1921 a bomb exploded at the shrine to the Virgin of Guadalupe, destroying part of the altar but not the sacred image. In 1923 Obregón expelled the apostolic delegate, Monsignor Ernesto Filippi, for taking part in a ceremony to build a monument to Christ the King on Cubilete Hill at the geographic center of the country near Silao, Guanajuato. The following year the Eucharistic Congress of October 1924 appeared to flout aspects of the law, and the president directed the attorney general of the republic to investigate and punish those involved. These incidents would be regarded as fairly mild compared to what occurred during Calles's regime.

The conflict must be placed in context. Nineteenth-century politics pitted liberalism against religious practices deeply ingrained in the everyday life of the vast majority of the lower class. The liberal attack on clerical influence in politics, Church ownership of vast properties, and religious fashioning of the national culture sought to remove the Church from everyday life and create a secular society and government. It became an issue of control. The distance between the two could have been bridged in the 1920s but the revolutionaries insisted on being the dominant voice in all spheres of political and social life. As

President Obregón wrote to the bishops after the expulsion of Filippi, "the high Catholic clergy have not sensed the transformation . . . in the minds of the people toward a modern (i.e., revolutionary) outlook." Obregón expressed his regrets that the Church refused to see that the "two programs could well cooperate" in the government's program because of its "essentially Christian and humanitarian" character.[2]

With President Calles, the relationship continued to deteriorate. The new president determined to give a secular character to everyday life. His effort to end Roman Catholic religious practices and influence resulted in what was termed "socialist education." This teaching ridiculed the faith as it taught literacy, mathematics, physical education, and practical skills such as gardening. In some states, especially Tabasco and Sonora, socialist education resulted in youth groups dedicated to iconoclastic programs that involved burning images of saints and even burning church buildings. Calles pressured the rural school program to become increasingly anticlerical. His policy soon resulted in clashes in remote zones between representatives of the revolutionary government and the Roman Catholic Church, priests, and teachers, with local people caught in the middle.

The president supported the creation of a national church, subject to the government's control, not to Rome's. The Mexican Apostolic Church, headed by a patriarch, did not recognize the Vatican's authority and declared celibacy immoral and illegal. Use of a corn tortilla instead of a wheat communion wafer and mescal in place of wine had deep symbolic significance. The government eventually assigned the Church of Corpus Christi to the Mexican Church. Its prominent location on Avenida Juárez across from the Alameda (#44) served as a public affront to the Catholic clergy. The archbishop José Mora y del Río of Mexico City issued an interdict forbidding Catholics to enter the building. Late in the year the state of Tabasco ordered that only married priests could conduct services. All state governors received the authority to decide how many priests could function in their state. Requirements to register, prohibition of appearing in public in clerical robes, and banning of foreign priests followed. The alarmed church hierarchy believed that Calles had implemented a strategic plan rather than just tactical harassment. The Church prelates declared that they would not accept the anticlerical articles of the Constitution of 1917, making confrontation almost certain. Rome dispatched a representative to attempt to arrange a reasonable compromise. Conciliation failed.

The Cristero Rebellion

In July 1926 the unthinkable happened. The Church, which had conducted its religious responsibilities from the moment Cortez had set foot on the Mexican coast in 1519, went on strike. Crowds in Mexico City lined up to receive last-minute confessions, hurried church marriages, confirmations, and baptisms before the suspension took effect.

The strike and the closure of the churches lasted for three years. Calles declared it to be a struggle between the revolution and the forces of reaction, of the forces of light against those of darkness. The Liga Nacional Defensora de la Libertad Religiosa (National League for the Defense of Religious Liberty) declared an economic boycott, with mixed results. In some areas it had a brief economic impact but soon faded, as consumers returned to their former buying patterns. Closure of churches caused some scuffles with police in various parts of the country, while in others the authorities demanded only limited compliance. Labor union leaders from 180 organizations met personally with the president to offer their support, and in August a crowd of forty thousand workers gathered in the *zócalo* to back the government. The following month, with the opening of Congress, Calles reported that the administration had closed a number of Catholic schools and other institutions, as well as expelled foreign priests. The president earlier advised the Church that only three options presented themselves: abide by the constitution, appeal to Congress, or revolt. Subsequently, Congress rejected a petition by the hierarchy. The two remaining option appeared equally unpalatable. Breaking the stalemate appeared impossible.

The proponents of Catholic social action did not oppose the revolution's social reforms, but rejected the ideological opposition to the Church. They could neither understand nor tolerate a regime and its programs that aimed to create a people bereft of religion. The 1917 Constitution included provisions that nationalized property of the Church and stripped the clergy of political rights, as well as proposed limiting clergy in various ways (restricting the total number in each state and permitting only Mexican citizens to serve as clerics). These anti-Church provisions did not provoke serious reaction until President Calles initiated his anticlerical policies from 1924 to 1928. These efforts included a general campaign to restrict the Church and the clergy, and to introduce socialist education. In 1926, in response to government policies, lay Catholics from the capital city and western Mexico rebelled.

The Church steered clear of advocating violence, although ambiguous instructions from Rome seemed to accept resistance as a means of pressuring the government. Small-scale uprisings occurred in several states, from Jalisco to Oaxaca. Isolated villages in mountainous terrain could be taken without much difficultly. But actions such as burning schoolhouses and on occasion murdering the teacher, attacking symbols of the government, had a negative impact on urban public opinion. The Liga sent supplies and encouragement, and a few priests accompanied the rebels. By 1927 some twelve thousand Cristeros, as they called themselves, opposed the revolutionary troops. The Cristero Rebellion continued as Catholic Defense League members battled official government troops. Even when the local clergy directed their parishioners to put down their arms, many fought on. In this callous civil war, armed with the confidence of true believers, both sides saw compromise as weakness and armistice as apostasy. Moreover both religion and revolution served as a disguise for others with a variety of motives to use violence against their neighbors. The death toll from the bitter fighting during the three years from 1926 to 1929 has been dramatically underestimated, despite sensational stories in both the government and church press. An attack on the city of León in Guanajuato failed, forcing a change in tactics. Attacking trains yielded better results. An assault on the Mexico City–Laredo train resulted in the killing of the escorting troops and the seizure of money. A similar attack on the Mexico City–Guadalajara line killed some one hundred people, as all cars derailed. By the end of 1927 only random acts of defiance disturbed western Mexico. In the urban areas, the arrest of Liga and Catholic Youth League members weakened their effectiveness. By then Calles had ordered many of the bishops to leave the country. Most of them took up residence in San Antonio, Texas. Sporadic murders revealed the ongoing campaigns of militant revolutionaries and the equally militant churchmen. The violence continued for two decades until a massacre of Church sympathizers in Leon, Guanajuato, in 1946.

On a lovely afternoon in November 1927, ex-president Obregón and two companions drove through Chapultepec Park in Mexico City. Suddenly a car pulled alongside and three bombs hit Obregón's Cadillac, followed by several shots. The attempted assassination failed, but left General Obregón covered with blood. A chase by his escorts resulted in the capture of the two assailants. It was discovered that a clergyman, Father Miguel Pro, had sold the automobile several days earlier, and the surviving assassins vaguely provide some links to Pro and his two brothers. The case of Fr. Miguel Pro Juárez SJ had a more profound negative impact on international public opinion than Cristero activity in the countryside. The devout Father Pro, involved in providing secret religious services in Mexico City, courted martyrdom. It is not clear that he played a major role in the event that led to his highly publicized and photographed execution by a firing squad. Nevertheless Calles made it plain that he wanted an example made of the Pros and the bomb throwers, without bothering about legalities. The executions conducted at the police station before a crowd of onlookers spared only the young Pro brother Humberto, saved by a last-minute telephone call from Calles. Photographs of the harsh proceedings circulated widely. At the moment of Father Pro's execution he shouted, "*Viva Cristo Rey*!"[3] He has recently been recognized as a saint of the Church.

A Yaqui revolt offered a diversion from the religious turmoil. An attack on a train, carrying Obregón, among other passengers, began what the government vowed to be an effort to put down the Yaquis once and for all. The 1926–1927 campaign seemed straightforward and understandable compared to the murky motivation of the Church-state conflict. While the Yaqui revolt did not threaten the north, it reminded many that other problems faced the country.

The public in the United States, including faithful Catholics, did not understand the underlying causes of the conflict, and investors in particular worried about instability. Washington made it known that they supported the Mexican government but only as long as it abided by the agreements on private property. Relations with the United States over subsoil issues and the religious war threatened to deteriorate into intervention, economic war, or worse. A way out of the mess came from an unexpected source.

Dwight W. Morrow, a corporation lawyer, partner in the banking firm of J. P. Morgan, accepted the nomination of President Coolidge, once his college roommate at Amherst, to be ambassador to Mexico. Coolidge named Morrow to replace the abrasive James Sheffield, an ambassador (1924–1927) who believed that threats and insults were effectual in dealing with the "Bolshevik" leaders of Mexico. During the same years that Sheffield was ambassador, Morrow had sat on banking commissions that dealt with Mexican loans and finances. His appointment as ambassador initially received a mixed reaction. The communist newspaper *El Machete* saw it as proof that Wall Street directed U.S. foreign policy. Others expected that Morrow might come first and that the U.S. Marines would follow. Before taking up his post Ambassador Morrow made several speeches before U.S. audiences, praising Mexico's leaders and indicating respect for the country's sovereignty as well as its culture. He also examined diplomatic files on the outstanding issues between the two republics. As a result of his advance preparation and fulsome words the Mexicans greeted this arrival with relief. Morrow's diplomacy fitted in with the importance of art and culture to the revolution, to efforts to create cultural ties across groups and regions. Morrow may not have been fully aware that he had tapped into the one area that remained open, even vulnerable, to a foreigner willing to embrace the revolutionary aesthetic. His friendship with Diego Rivera, seen by many in the United States as a dangerous communist, indicated that he subordinated ideology to art.

Morrow's obvious fascination with Mexico and its artisans and artistic creativity enchanted officials.[4] Assisted by René d'Harnoncourt, who subsequently became the director of the Museum of Modern Art in New York, Morrow amassed an amazing collection. With items from this collection, Harnoncourt organized one of the first exhibitions of Mexican art at New York's Metropolitan Museum of Art in 1930–1931. Sponsored by the Carnegie Corporation, the exhibit traveled to thirteen major cities, from Boston to San Antonio.

The ambassador made it clear that he considered the regulation of petroleum to be a domestic issue to be handled in Mexican courts. A relieved President Calles then saw to it that the Mexican Supreme Court decided in favor of U.S. oil companies. Both sides got what they wanted. Calles strengthened his domestic authority and Morrow disposed of a diplomatic problem that threatened to plunge both sides into an unwanted confrontation.

The ambassador also nudged both the Church and Calles toward a compromise. A secret meeting between Calles and a representative of the Catholic Church failed to resolve the issue, nevertheless the fact that it occurred at all made it possible to envision an eventual solution. Calles and the ambassador often met over breakfast. Because of the so-called ham-and-eggs meetings, close personal relations developed between the ambassador and the president, although Calles always breakfasted on popcorn dusted with chocolate.

Such pleasant relations collapsed in 1930 when Morrow ran for a New Jersey seat in the U.S. Senate. Alexander McNab, the former military attaché, publicly praised Morrow's manipulation of Mexican leaders and his assistance to cabinet ministers. These commendations in U.S. newspaper accounts became headline news in Mexico. Subsequently Morrow's telephone calls went unanswered, letters were returned, and doors closed in front of the discredited ambassador. Leaving this post to take up a seat in Senate came as a relief. Nevertheless, his efforts moved the Cristero struggle toward resolution.

Other Forces of Change

The revolutionaries opened new political and economic opportunities with their victories over the Porfirian regime and those who wanted it to continue. More significant than their specific reform programs was their creation of a consciousness of possibilities open to individuals who dared to follow their dreams. Of course many found only disappointments but others managed to achieve their hopes. Besides the revolutionary destruction of the Porfirian regime (with its Victorian cosmopolitan views), three other major forces made opportunities more apparent for Mexicans. These were domestic urbanization (begun during the Porfirian years), international campaigns for women's political rights, and the rise of the mass media, particularly recorded music and movies. These movements or forces combined with the revolutionary social changes to establish what is now labeled the Golden Age of urban popular culture in Mexico. The cities, especially the capital, grew in population during the worst fighting of the revolution and the incessant violence that persisted during campaigns for reforms. Cities offered not only security but also the prospect of a new life that included escape from the daily drudgery of subsistence agriculture, suffocating regulation by traditional communities, and the stifling dullness of the abandoned countryside. Instead of wondering where the roads and the railways went, country people, especially the young, followed them and discovered urban life. For many this meant poverty, discrimination, and survival through the outlaw economy of street vendors, petty criminals, and unlicensed prostitutes, whom the police and other officials regularly exploited. Nevertheless for many others it meant unimaginable excitement and opportunities, new jobs, indoor plumbing, and the dazzling entertainment of movies, radio, stage shows, and recorded music.

During the 1920s both official and unofficial cultural projects flourished, from the national murals inspired by José Vasconcelos to the adopting of fads from Europe and the United States, such as flappers. The official campaign for cultural change had a cosmopolitan sensibility and was based on an unstated commitment to take the best programs in the world and remake society. This motivation resulted in the formation of the Ministry of Public Education's Commission for Indigenous Research, an organization that sent anthropologist Moisés Sáenz traveling through Guatemala, Ecuador, Peru, and Bolivia, collecting information on programs that had succeeded in integrating indigenous peoples into wider society. Moisés Sáenz's journey resulted in experimental communities, beginning with the creation of a permanent cultural mission in Actopan, Hidalgo. Another example of this drive to obtain information on social experiments came when Plutarco Calles made a tour through Europe to observe the social programs of Spanish and Italian fascism and Scandinavian socialism. His conclusions found their way into many of his presidential programs. Vasconcelos, in devising his sweeping popular education program, drew inspiration from a variety of international sources, perhaps none greater than John Dewey who visited him in Mexico, as he fashioned his policies for cultural change.

Unofficially Mexicans seized the opportunity to express their freedom. Flappers, called "Las Pelonas" (short-haired girls) for their bobbed hair, caused a sensation in different parts of the capital and some were met by rock-throwing adults offended by their appearance. Stage productions, especially at the Iris Theater, featured scenes of this new culture and resulted in the adoption of the term the "Ciudad de las Tandas," (City of Scenes) to describe it. The popularity of recorded music inspired Ernesto Baptisa in 1921 to establish Peerless Records in Mexico City. At first, Peerless recordings of public songs, including *posadas* and boleros, were pressed under a contract with Gennett Records in Richmond, Indiana, but by the early 1940s Peerless had its own production center in Mexico. Peerless sold records across Mexico, the southwest United States, and elsewhere in Latin America. During this time, popular interest in music shifted from operas and *corridos* to boleros, and this change was reinforced with the introduction of radio. In short time records, radio, and movies turned singer-actors such as Agustín Lara into stars. The new urban culture reflected a sense of opportunity and freedom, opportunity created by the revolution and the revolutionary regime.

Nothing reflected the cultural change more than the blossoming of romance. Beginning in the 1920s, the revolutionary generation dismissed flowers, handkerchiefs, and flirtatious conversations through windows (called "playing the bear"). Instead they turned to public displays of affection, especially kissing. Once the private expression of lovers' intimacy, it became the explicit metaphor of the new age. To the outrage of Church and social conservatives, songs, movies, photographs, and postcards all focused on the kiss. On street corners, park benches, movie theaters, and other public places, the revolutionary generation kissed.

Suggested Reading

Bailey, David C. *¡Viva Cristo Rey! The Cristero Rebellion and the Church-State Conflict in Mexico*. Austin: University of Texas Press, 1974.

Buchenau, Jurgen. *Plutarco Elías Calles and the Mexican Revolution*. Boulder CO: Rowman & Littlefield, 2006.

Dulles, John W. F. *Yesterday in Mexico: A Chronicle of the Revolution, 1919–1936*. Austin: University of Texas Press, 1961.

Harris, Charles, and Louis Ray Sadler. *El Paso and the Mexican Revolution*. Albuquerque: University of New Mexico Press, 2008.

Wilkie, James W., and Albert L. Michaels. *Revolution in Mexico: Years of Upheaval, 1910–1940*. New York: Alfred A. Knopf, 1969.

3

REELECTION AND CONTESTED SUFFRAGE

(*Previous page*) 3. Photograph of Lázaro Cárdenas and mariachis. Lázaro Cárdenas traveled across Mexico during his presidential campaign. He utilized mariachi bands to connect audiences to his populist programs. Family photograph of the Marmolejo Family, used with permission.

The Election of 1928

General and former president Alvaro Obregón had gone back to garbanzo bean cultivation in 1924 after assuring the presidential election of his friend General Calles. He relinquished the office with reluctance, understanding that any attempt to hold on to the presidency would be contested by a horde of ambitious generals who would surely evoke the almost sacred mantra: "Effective Suffrage and No Reelection." Nevertheless, Obregón maintained close contact with influential congressmen and kept a critical eye on political events. Out of office one could accomplish scarcely anything, he complained.

As he contemplated the problem of succession, Calles preferred the CROM leader Morones, allegedly because of the central importance of labor. Obregón did not share that view, and consequently Calles put forward the possibility of Gen. Arnulfo R. Gómez, the chief of military operations in Veracruz. Obregón suggested that his former minister of war, Gen. Francisco R. Serrano, might be a good selection, although it is not clear that he actually believed that Serrano could perform in the high office. General Serrano had a gambling problem and a fondness for nightlife. Subsequently Obregón pronounced that Gómez and Serrano were both unacceptable. After some thought, he decided that he would run again. He interpreted "no reelection" to mean "no consecutive terms," but to clear up any misperception,

Congress amended the constitution to permit nonconsecutive terms. Another amendment lengthened the term in office to six years. Calles was aware that to deny the ex-president the office would be dangerous and fruitless in the end, as Obregón had the support of most of the generals. Others worried that Obregón intended to be another Porfirio Díaz, with one term after another or perhaps alternating in office with Calles. Both Gómez and Serrano announced their candidacy, making it a three-way race. Opponents of Obregón believed that his violation of the no-reelection principle gave them the moral high ground and that others would rally to them. The resurrection of Francisco Madero's defunct Anti-reeleccionista party emphasized the issue—and Arnulfo Gómez became its candidate. When Gómez declared in Puebla that Obregón supporters should be sent to the Tres Marías penal colony or put two meters below ground for going against the no-reelection principle, it was obvious that the contest would become violent.

Gómez miscalculated the public's reaction to the issue, making the same mistake as Madero by assuming that politics, not socio-economic concerns, motivated the lower classes and that an aroused nation would make it impossible to impose Obregón. In the end, in another miscalculation, Serrano decided on a revolt. Only one-fourth of the army joined him and the trap set for Calles and Obregón failed. Under orders from Calles, Gen. Claudio Fox executed the hapless Serrano and thirteen other conspirators caught on the Cuernavaca highway, in what became known as the Huitzilac Massacre. Almost a month later federal troops arrested and shot to death General Gómez, Col. Francisco Gómez Vizcarra, and others in the cemetery at Coatepec, Veracruz.

The process of fatal subtraction left only Obregón, who won reelection handily. Ironically Obregón as president-elect boasted to Calles that he had proved that "the presidential palace is not necessarily the antechamber of the cemetery." At a celebratory dinner at La Bombilla, a fine restaurant in San Angel, on July 17, 1928, a sketch artist made his way around the tables until he reached Obregón. Pulling a revolver, he shot five times, hitting the president-elect twice, killing the hero of Celaya and many other bloody battles. The corpse lay in state in the National Palace. Lines of mourners and the curious filed past as alert soldiers watched and directed. Subsequently a funeral procession took place, with Calles and other high officials following the casket, and then Obregón's body was sent home to Sonora.

José de León Toral, the assassin, was interrogated—and tortured—at the General Inspectorate of Police. He proved to be a religious zealot, a close friend of the Pros, a supporter of the Cristeros, and a follower of a charismatic nun, Madre Conchita, who was also arrested. She willing admitted her inspirational role in the shooting. The trial of Toral and Madre Conchita became a huge public spectacle that ended with the execution of the assassin and the sentencing of Madre Conchita to thirty years on the island prison colony of the Tres Marias. An earlier plan to kill Calles or Obregón also came to light. This involved María Elena Manzano who intended to arm herself with a vial of poison to inject into her victim as they danced. Although she traveled to Celaya hoping for the right moment, Manzano failed to make the required close contact.

The 1928 presidential succession was a political crisis with all the contenders dead. Many believed that someone had orchestrated all the assassinations and that the true culprits would eventually be unmasked. Luis Morones, aware that such suspicion might center on him, hurriedly left Mexico City. A climate of betrayal and ambition that characterized the politics of revolutionary generals made rumors and paranoid conspiracy theories believable. As Calles commented to Obregón when he gave the orders to kill Serrano and Gómez, "They would have killed *us* had their plot succeeded." Others remembered that both Gómez and Serrano had served Obregón before they turned on their mentor.

Gen. Benjamin Hill, referred to sometimes as Obregón's missing right arm, had been eliminated eight years before. General Hill's fatal poisoning at a banquet in 1920—where Calles, also one of the honorees, had not been affected—immediately created gossip and speculation about the identity of the "Borgia." Eight years later many believed that it was Calles who had struck Obregón down.

Outgoing President Calles's authority had weakened as he prepared to leave office but after Obregón's death it almost disappeared. The Chamber of Deputies was filled with some Obregónistas who were angry at the president. Fortunately, some other well-known supporters of Obregón stepped in to defuse the crisis that threatened to explode into disorder and violence as legitimacy disappeared.

General Joaquin Amaro sternly warned the army to attend to its duty and Gen. Aarón Sáenz, of the Centro Director Obregónista, advised people to remain calm. Calles made public pronouncements promising to punish the assassins and assassination plotters. Cabinet resignations, notably that of Luis Morones, and new appointments, including Emilio Portes Gil as minister of internal affairs (Gobernación) brought the immediate situation under control. Nevertheless the problem of the presidency remained. The generals had mixed advice for Calles. A perfect solution for many, making the newly legal six-year term retroactive and thus extending Calles's term, would not be accepted by others with their own ambitions. The matter would have to be decided by Congress or a military rebellion. Calles ended speculation about his intentions with a pledge before Congress to step down at the end of his constitutional term and not seek reelection at any time in the future. At the same time he urged legislators to end the era of caudillos and create a truly democratic system. Laying aside the question of the president's sincerity, his address made it possible to move to the selection of a provisional president as provided by the constitution, although military action could not be discounted. Calles, with the acquiescence of the top generals, guided Congress in the selection process. The governor of Tamaulipas, Emilio Portes Gil, a strong supporter of Obregón, had been helpful to Calles after the assassination of the president-elect and seemed a prudent choice. Congress duly followed the outgoing president's preference and elected Portes Gil provisional president. Calles's new role as a statesman and advocate of democratic reforms shifted the focus from himself to Congress and the impending election of a president to finish Obregón's aborted term.

President Emilio Portes Gil

In 1929 Portes Gil made it known that he wanted to resolve the government's dispute with the Church and he praised the declaration of the bishopric of Oaxaca's secretary that Catholics should respect government authorities. The president also made it clear that he did not hold the Church hierarchy responsible for Cristero violence. Moreover he asserted that the government would not persecute the clergy. He skillfully glossed over the unpleasant immediate past and indicated his openness to a resumption of Catholic services. Archbishop Leopoldo Ruiz y Flores responded at a press conference that men of goodwill could bridge their differences. Portes Gil indicated that he would be open to a meeting. Rome duly appointed Archbishop Ruiz y Flores the apostolic delegate to Mexico to arrange an end to the stalemate. U.S. Ambassador Morrow, briefed on the Church's position, did his best to assist, but both sides wanted a settlement and willingly accepted the assurance of goodwill in place of constitutional changes. Agreeing to disagree provided an exit from the lingering confrontation with an amnesty. Some fourteen thousand Cristeros took advantage of the opportunity and surrendered to federal troops. On Sunday June 30, 1929, church bells rang throughout the capital, calling the faithful to mass again for the first time since 1926.

President Portes Gil also faced another issue with future consequences. University students, many sympathetic to José Vasconcelos, began a general strike that deteriorated into violence. Closure of the National University followed. After fire fighters turned their hoses on the students the level of anger mounted. Police were summoned and several students were wounded in the first of a series of melees. Rather than escalate, Portes Gil withdrew the police and fire department and requested that the students formulate a list of grievances. After a receiving a series of impossible demands, the president sidestepped the issues to establish university autonomy. Setting up a new administrative structure with appropriate representation, including students, ended the matter. Portes Gil's popularity soared.

Largely overlooked at the time, a new, potentially powerful interest group emerged. A generation of university-educated individuals poised to enter professional careers coalesced around educator José Vasconcelos. As middle-class citizens they wanted political stability and a predictable future, but also a return to civilian rule with no multiple terms for presidents. All of this required wresting the country from the hands of revolutionary generals. At the same time Calles and other high officials, as Obregón had earlier, understood that they increasingly relied upon educated technocrats across a wide range of fields. How to bring them into the system and still maintain control posed a problem. It could not be solved by incorporating them into the army or the Rurales as had been the case of peasants and bandits in earlier days. Their time did not come for many years.

As the presidential election neared, one might have expected a political struggle between revolutionary factions backed by various generals, some violence, and perhaps a military rebellion. Calles had a different series of events in mind. He envisioned the formation of a strong party that could mobilize the population across the republic and provide a powerful national role for the ex-president. He observed how Morones used the Regional Confederation of Mexican Workers (CROM) to exert influence and shape policy. He thought of an even more powerful national party able to bring different groups together, not just workers. The idea of a party-based system had been advocated by the reform-minded Cientificos during the Díaz regime in 1892 and 1903. Obregón more recently had suggested the advisability of an elected party and an out-of-office party, with the latter funded by the government. Up to that point most parties had formed around individuals, tended to be local rather than national, and lasted only briefly, with their place taken by others equally as fleeting. Calles commissioned a study of politics in the United States, England, and France to provide some ideas. The grand conviction of bridging difference between Callistas and Obregónistas, curbing personal politics, limiting military participation, and carrying out social programs, seemed an achievable goal.

The Partido Nacional Revolucionario (PNR) encompassed all revolutionary groups—labor, peasants (campesinos), civil servants, and the military. The party laid claim to the liberal mantle of Benito Juarez and his Constitution of 1857, the Madero revolt against Díaz, the Constitution of 1917, and various revolutionary programs, including agrarian reform. Besides an all-inclusive ideology, the PNR demanded strict party discipline. Over time the party developed a reward structure that moved members up the ladder within the government or the party based on their loyalty, ability, and performance. The PNR newspaper, *El Nacional*, supported the party and reported the news with an approved slant. The newspaper referred to General Calles as "Jefe Máximo de la Revolución," a title that conveyed a Benito-Juarez-like mantle and implied moral authority to direct the unfolding of the revolution.

In an inspired touch, the party held its inaugural session in Querétaro, the birthplace of the Constitution of 1917, in the same building where the document was signed. The party went on to put forth as their candidate Pascual Ortiz Rubio. Fresh from diplomatic service in Europe, Ortiz Rubio had few enemies and a solid record of loyalty to Obregón and Calles. The other possibility, Gen. Aarón Sáenz, initially preferred by Calles, had fought beside Obregón and served as his chief of staff. The calculated switch to Ortiz Rubio rested on the belief that his candidacy might make it more difficult for disaffected generals to mount a successful military revolt. As others pointed out, Sáenz as a pro-business advocate as well as a Protestant could easily be portrayed as an antirevolutionary, particularly among campesinos. His apparent willingness to cooperate fully with Calles also upset Obregónistas.

The revolt that accompanied nearly all presidential elections occurred on March 3, 1929, with the idea of replacing Portes Gil with Gen. José Gonzalo Escobar as provisional president. A significant facet of the plan called for a quick move on the capital and seizing Calles, President Portes Gil, and Gen. Joaquín Amaro, minister of war. The rebels' "Plan of Hermosillo" listed serious complaints against Calles and named General Escobar as the "Supreme Chief of the Army of Revolutionary Renewal." The propaganda had the same ring as that directed against Victoriano Huerta by the Constitutionalists following the death of Madero. At this critical moment, General Amaro, injured in a polo match, went to the United States for treatment at the Mayo Clinic in Minnesota. President Portes Gil named General Calles war minister in Amaro's stead to direct operations against the Escobar revolt. Calles controlled at least 70 percent of the federal army and most campesinos, including a division of five thousand pulled together in San Luis Potosí, as well as urban workers. Once the rebellion in Veracruz was put down, Calles moved rapidly north, using airplanes. Those who surrendered to Calles and his government forces received money, pardons, and rail tickets back to their villages. Some two thousand died in the rebellion, while most of the leaders escaped across the border into the United States.

General Calles used his military success to remind the nation that the political failure of the revolution contrasted glaringly with its successful social reforms. In his view political failure could be remedied only by political parties and in particular by the PNR. The complete triumph of the revolution depended on a workable political structure. Strengthening the republic's institutions became one of the revolution's principal objectives as interpreted by Calles. This involved a shift of power from the presidency to an institutional structure controlled by party members theoretically subordinate to the PNR. The emergence of party bosses provided a role for ambitious people such as Calles.

In 1931 the PNR established its own radio station XE-PNR (later XEFO) with the purpose of mass political mobilization and formation of a national consensus. By the early 1930s regulations prohibited radio stations from offering independent views, reserving political commentary exclusively for government officials.[1] To reach as many listeners as possible the PNR distributed radios and loudspeakers to villages and urban areas. President Portes Gil ordered mandatory federal payroll deductions to finance the party, which sought to tie all Mexicans into a fabricated nationalistic culture, one that the PNR portrayed as reflecting the values of the revolution.

Mexico is unique in that the government created a party, but

Calles did not have in mind shared rule between the government and the party following the Soviet model. Nevertheless the president's ability to impose his successor on the country strengthened as the party became a means of organizing popular support for a president's handpicked candidate.

The administration also attempted to implement more of the social changes mandated by the constitution. Two major efforts at enabling this were 1931 Penal Code and the 1931 Labor Law. Both these had significant effects. Although some tinkering had occurred over the previous decades, 1931 marked the first major revision of the 1872 Penal Code, with changes made regarding the relationship between married couples, the rights of married women, and the protection of women in adulterous relationships. The rights of children received some recognition as well. The Labor Code of the same year moved toward the implementation of safety regulations, minimum wages, and some benefits. This law was particularly important for recognizing women as workers and formalizing their rights as well.

Written references to the CROM and other labor organizations often imply male workers, yet in some ways the most striking change in the nature of the urban workforce involved women, who followed the expansion of telephone service across the capital city and to other parts of the country. Young and usually single, many women took jobs as phone operators. The telephone workers' union (Sindicato de Telefonistas de la República Mexicana) represented the largest group of women in the formal economy. Along with the Pelonas, female revolutionary veterans, and recent migrants to the city, these telephone operators adopted new lifestyles, modeled in part on comic books, radio broadcasts, talking movies, and recorded music. They were *las chicas moderna*, modern young women.

Mexico City became a revolutionary capital, with changes in street and building names to reflect new revolutionary heroes and to excise the old regime, new architecture styles, and enlarged government offices for the new and larger agencies charged with carrying out social programs. The presidential palace grew to two stories to provide office space for the increasing number of bureaucrats. Mexico City grew in power like a new Rome as it drew people to its wealth and opportunity.

The nation became increasingly cosmopolitan. In 1927 the Southern Pacific Railroad connected Nogales, Sonora, at the U.S. border, with Guadalajara, over a thousand miles to the south, tying Nogales into the national network centered on the capital. That same year telephone service connected Mexico City with the United States and Canada. Domestic phone lines reached into several northern states although connections required a wait of half an hour or more. The transition from telegraph to voice had a positive affect on political and business communications. In another development, in the interest of commerce, President Obregón encouraged the establishment of more radio stations. It quickly became evident that radio had political possibilities that required attention. A 1926 law had defined the airways as a national resource subject to concessions limited to citizens and awarded by the government. The law prohibited broadcasts that endangered public order or national security. Subsequent laws enacted in 1931 and 1932 required that all broadcasts be in Spanish and originate from locations within Mexico. In addition, radio stations had to broadcast government messages without charge, including the health department's daily ten-minute instructions on public health concerns.

Outside the capital, the revolutionaries made changes as well. Road construction, previously all but ignored in favor of railroads, now became critical as a secondary feeder network for railways. Only the highway east from Mexico City to Puebla and the one west to Toluca met reasonable standards. Most of country used rutted roads that made travel difficult, time-consuming, costly, and dangerous. The Comisión Nacional de Caminos (National Highway Commission) established in 1925, funded in part by a gasoline tax and supplemented by the treasury, spent a million pesos a month, with some ten thousand men working under the direction of León Salinas and other engineers. By the end of 1927, twenty-three million pesos had gone into road construction. That same year the Comisión Nacional de Irrigación, directed by the agricultural ministry, set a target of half a million hectares of irrigated land. They reached only half that acreage but this changed the nature of agriculture in arid northern Mexico. Dams captured storm-driven rain that swept across mountain barriers and ran off land, too parched to penetrate. Irrigation in turn allowed the commercial vegetable cultivation that exists today for the export market.

A changing conception of time and distance, coupled with an extension of the reach of the federal government through railways, telegraph, telephone, and radio, altered the relationship between the federal administration and the states. The railroad had linked some remote parts of the country and enabled access to foreign markets, but the road-building program of this era connected rural areas to regional cities and the emergence of bus service then made transport easier and faster. Aviation, psychologically jarring around the world, had even more impact on a country that was still living in the nineteenth century in some places. Charles A. Lindbergh's conquest of the Atlantic seemed to shrink the ocean into a large pond. His appearance in Mexico, arranged by Ambassador Morrow, caused a sensation. Lindbergh met the ambassador's daughter, Anne, whom he married. Not to be left behind, Mexican aviators also established records.

Roberto Fierro made a fourteen-hour nonstop flight from Mexicali to Mexico City in 1928. Emilio Carranza flew from Mexico City to Washington that same year but died when his plane was struck by lighting as he was taking off for the return trip. Carranza's funeral was a national day of mourning, as he was recognized as Mexico's greatest pilot at the time. The Central American tour of Pablo Sidar drew awed crowds in 1929 to marvel at his daring and watch takeoffs and landings. Unfortunately Sidar, too, was a crash victim. On a nonstop goodwill flight to Argentina, Sidar and copilot Pablo Rovirosa died when their plane, the *Morelos*, went down off the coast of Costa Rica in 1930. Their recovered bodies lay in state in the National Palace. That same year Roberto Fierro flew from Los Angeles to New York, then nonstop to Mexico City. Mexican aviation represented the country's participation in new technology that pushed back of the frontiers of time and space. Air travel changed Mexicans' perceptions of the world beyond the national borders and changed views of Mexico internationally in the eyes of foreigners who admired the country's fliers.

In the midst of revolutionary change, the world intruded disastrously in Mexico in 1929. Foreign investment in manufacturing and mining dropped to insignificant levels. Moreover the deepening worldwide depression threatened the existence of liberal democracies and encouraged self-contained economic development. Italy, Germany, and the Soviet Union organized their economic response around government initiatives. The United States, confused, seemed unable to halt the economic slide or revive trade. A world economic conference in London in 1933 failed to move beyond finger pointing.

Balancing Power: Presidents Pascual Ortiz Rubio (1930–1932) and Abelardo Rodríguez (1932–1934) and the PNR (1929–1938)

The selection of Pascual Ortiz Rubio as the PNR's presidential candidate did not heal the divisions in Congress. Two factions, the "Whites" and the "Reds," struggled for control of official patronage. Calles tipped the balance between the factions, as the losers remained disgruntled. Rumors of a planned assassination circulated. Coming on the heels of Obregón's death, such an event would have been disastrous to Calles's attempt to establish political stability. Ortiz Rubio won a decisive victory over challenger José Vasconcelas, and additional security resulted in a trouble-free inauguration at the National Stadium. After returning to the National Palace, President Ortiz Rubio, his wife, niece, and a staff officer left for a relaxing ride in Chapultepec Park. As they left the palace, six shots were fired toward them by a young man named Daniel Flores, and the president was wounded but not fatally. Quickly captured, Flores was found to have some connection with the Vasconcelistas but no direct ties. Efforts to find the plotters of the assassination, by now a political category more important than assassins themselves, proved fruitless. Rumors revolved, speculating about who might have had something to gain by such a deed. Portes Gil, Calles, and others were suspected, but with no solid evidence. Partly in frustration, those connected with Vasconcelos's Anti-reelection Party bore the blunt of arrests and interrogations at the barracks of the Fifty-first Cavalry Regiment commanded by Gen. Maximino Avila Camacho. On the orders of Gen. Eulogio Ortiz, commander of the Valley of Mexico Military District, some one hundred Vasconcelistas died without any evidence that they plotted to assassinate the president or, more important, to derail the PNR as they were charged with having done. The victims were taken to Topilejo on the Mexico City–Cuernavaca road, hanged, and buried in graves that they had been forced to dig, satisfying for some the blood lust and frustration aroused by the election of 1929. These events delayed the emergence of a new generation of university-trained politicians eager to displace revolutionary generals. Vasconcelos retreated into bitterness as the government quashed press coverage of the executions and took no action against the perpetrators. The government suggested that Vasconcelos leave Mexico and not return, and so he did—beginning a six-year exile that would be ended by Lázaro Cárdenas in 1936. Meanwhile, government inaction provided a warning to others that any challenge to the PNR might be fatal.

The 1930s delivered a series of shocks worldwide. The collapse of world trade following the U.S. stock market crash of 1929 unleashed latent strains of extremism as frightened societies moved to the right. Self-sufficiency and internal development replaced a discredited trade system and the desire for control of resources reinvigorated and legitimized colonialism under many guises. Many wondered if liberal democracies could survive politically in the face of a self-confident European fascism. Japan moved into Manchuria as it began to set up its "Co-Prosperity Sphere," while Italy advanced into Africa, seizing Ethiopia. Germany recklessly broke the terms of the Versailles treaty to reoccupy the Rhineland. Internationally the situation seemed grim and there were even more shocks to come.

On a national level Mexico experienced poor harvests, largely a result of unfavorable weather, with potentially devastating social repercussions. Commodity demand dropped as the U.S. and overseas markets shriveled. Metals, minerals, and agriculture brought in sharply lower revenues, with negative consequences for employment, taxes and investments. The government responded with economic measures that included a balanced budget, but this aggravated unemployment and curtailed consumption. Money in circulation dropped, further contracting the economy. In 1931 it became evident that the budgetary shortfall amounted to eighty million pesos, almost one-third of the budget. Wage cuts and drastic reduction in the number of government employees reduced the shortfall by sixty million, but this still required tax increases and revision of tariffs to achieve a balanced budget. In 1931 Calles, now president of the Bank of Mexico, introduced a monetary law that made the silver peso the standard unit and demonetized gold. In order to keep the value of the silver peso stable, restrictions on new minting of silver coins further reduced money in circulation, with predictable deflationary economic consequences. Government employees often did not receive their pay on schedule and those outside the capital had to wait even longer. Schoolteachers in San Luis Potosí waited over three months for their wages. The unemployed staged huge demonstrations and the CROM demanded that the government take action to stop the closing of factories. Railroad employment dropped by almost thirty-nine thousand from 1929 to 1932.

Fortunately Alberto J. Pani, Mexico's ambassador to France, returned to accept the position of finance minister. Pani understood the monetary problem. He removed control of coinage from the Bank of Mexico and ordered the mint to turn out silver coins as fast as possible. A monetary law established 1932 reduced the silver content of coins, increasing monetary liquidity that restored some economic confidence.

In rural areas, workers who had supplemented their income with casual labor found little employment and even lower wages. Unemployed miners returned to villages, swelling the number of those seeking work. The one hope remaining was land reform, as Calles went to Europe in 1929 to study its agricultural experiences. He returned convinced that the division of land had crippled French productivity. As modern machinery needed large-scale operations to increase yields and cut costs, division of land appeared counterproductive. In 1929 government redistributed slightly more than one million hectares of land, but after Calles had communicated his negative conclusions to the Ortiz Rubio cabinet, the amount of land turned over to campesinos fell and in 1932 reached only one-third of that redistributed in 1929. In addition a 1931 law set time limits on requests of land. The calibrated redistribution of land necessary to achieve peace in the countryside had been cut to the bone, prematurely as it turned out.

President Ortiz Rubio found it increasingly difficult to function, with a cabinet subordinated to Calles rather than to him. He had failed to earn the respect of his cabinet at the start of his presidency and appeared politically inept. Most cabinet officials openly indicated their loyalty to Calles and did not hesitate to clear government initiatives with the general first. Pani, perhaps the most brilliant of his generation, became alienated from the president over allegations that road contracts appeared to have involved a payoff to the president, among others. In addition rumors that Ortiz Rubio made disparaging comments about him annoyed the finance minister who failed to understand that a frustrated and weak president could only mutter in the shadows of power. Pani went to Calles and threatened to resign, only to be told that an occasion would present itself shortly but meanwhile to remain in the cabinet. Clearly Calles had decided that the president would have to be replaced. To force the president's resignation, Calles instructed his cohorts not to accept any cabinet posts in the government. In response to Dr. Puig Casauranc's relaying Calles's decision to him, the panicked president wondered how he could find competent individuals to staff his administration, people who were not linked to Calles. In fact he could not. He attempted to govern by drawing on Supreme Court justices unaffiliated with General Calles—and this worked briefly. Ortiz Rubio resigned after Calles approved of the way he had worded his announcement. In his statement he referred to the need to consolidate the "Calles Doctrine," defined as a strengthening of institutions and making Mexico a land of laws. To be on the safe side Ortiz Rubio and his family departed by train for the U.S. border, almost at the moment his resignation came before Congress.

Calles had time to contemplate a suitable candidate to replace Ortiz Rubio. Pani, first on Calles's list, declined, noting that he did not want to be president as a result of Calles's intimidation of Congress. Of the other two candidates, Gen. Joaquin Amaro and Gen. Abelardo Rodríguez, the latter appeared more acceptable to the PNR as appointed interim president to complete the term. As president, General Rodríguez made it plain to all that he intended to be his own man. Although it is not clear how much the former president's failure to command the presidency may have been due to his personality, President Rodríguez intended to be a fully functioning executive. He made an example out of a shocked Finance Minister Pani by requesting his resignation almost immediately. He instructed other cabinet members not to take up matters with Calles unless he so instructed them. As a revolutionary he claimed equal status with the Jefe Máximo. To underscore the authority of the president and the supportive role assigned the ex-president, General Calles assumed the post of interim finance minister. A similar outcome involved the arrival of Josephus Daniels, the new U.S. ambassador, who arrived under the impression that Calles called all the shots in Mexico. Consequently he arrived bearing a letter from Franklin D. Roosevelt congratulating Calles on Mexico's progress under his guidance. A presentation banquet with appropriate attendees seemed appropriate for an occasion calculated to cement relations between the new ambassador and the alleged iron man. President Rodríguez informed his cabinet that he would dismiss anyone who attended. As president, he said, he should have received the FDR letter. A determined Rodríguez refused to allow his authority to be compromised. Calles pleaded illness and cancelled the banquet. In an exchange of official letters with Daniels, President Rodríguez pointedly explained that he handled all administrative and political matters. As the ambassador later wrote, everyone—including Calles—knew that "the man in Chapultepec Castle [the presidential residence] was the president of Mexico."[2]

Daniels's appointment in 1933 caused a stir in Mexico. He had served in the Wilson administration as secretary of the navy and the young FDR had served as his undersecretary. In that capacity Daniels issued the orders to seize the port of Veracruz in 1914. President Abelardo L. Rodríguez only reluctantly accepted his appointment.[3] The self-styled shirt-sleeved diplomat soon overcame that embarrassment. He did not speak a word of Spanish and did not drink alcohol, but had all the skills of a genial, warm, "good ol' boy" able to form friendships with people from all levels of society. A staunch Methodist, he came under suspicion among U.S. Catholics for being too accepting of Mexican anticlericalism, particularly in education policy. What may have been a negative in the United States had the reverse impact in Mexico, although the charge appeared ill-founded.[4]

Once General Rodríguez had firmly established his presidential authority, he addressed the problem of wages. Calles opposed increasing wages because he believed that it would cause prices to rise, undercutting any gains. Former President Portes Gil had struggled with ways to increase the purchasing power of wages without much success. When he had governed Baja California, President Rodríguez had instituted a minimum wage of four pesos per day in the border state. Baja California's economy, with its casinos, racetracks, bars, and brothels, linked to San Diego and Los Angeles, easily carried a minimum wage. He intended to do the same nationally. He established a commission to study wages across the country. The president considered the situation of the working class to be the fundamental one that he faced. Congress passed legislation amending labor laws, including a three-peso minimum wage, although the actual wages generally already exceeded that amount.

The agrarian problem also received attention. By 1933 the amount of land distributed fell to a low not seen since 1922. In addition the federal government did not confirm many provincial grants made by state governments. President Rodriguez created an autonomous Agrarian Department separate from the Agricultural Ministry that appeared more interested in commercial agriculture. Within the new department an Agrarian Consultative Committee, meeting twice a week, cleared away the backlog. In addition the president ended the use of injunctions by landholders to stop expropriation proceedings. As a result, within six months 1,218,000 more hectares had been distributed. Nevertheless Rodríguez preferred individual ownership rather than communal *ejidos*. Meeting the objections of many critics of land reform, that it imperiled food supplies and exports, he increased funding for the Agrarian Credit Bank to assist in getting redistributed land into production.

A new Labor Department, separate from the Ministry of Commerce and Industry, reported directly to the president. Rodríguez instructed government officials to follow the guidelines of the 1933

Six-year Plan, ratified by the PNR at the end of 1933, that called for more government intervention in economic matters. The Labor Department made all contracts with closed shops, allowing unions to specify who could be hired and fired. The president personally intervened to settle strikes with binding arbitration, including ones in the petroleum industry, settling workplace issues and wages usually in favor of strikers. The workweek declined to 46.5 hours and paid holidays increased. The new power of labor caused intense competition between unions. Vicente Lombardo Toledano broke with Morones to form the General Confederation of Workers (Confederación de Trabajadores Mexicanos). A National Chamber of Labor proved unable to contain labor rivalry. President Rodríguez's two years in office consolidated government patronage of labor, and the next step would be to extend political control.

In 1933 General Calles believed that the next president should adopt a more revolutionary bent in reaction to the worldwide economic situation. The apparent collapse of capitalism in 1929 and the crisis of confidence of liberal democracy required rethinking Mexico's direction. FDR's plunge into federal government projects seemed a good model and Mexico, on the advice of the undersecretary of finance, Eduardo Suarez, adopted Keynesian policies. In order to expand the reach of the revolution Calles drafted a six-year plan, drawing on concrete data from every department in the government. The PNR's national convention scheduled for the end of 1933 in Querétaro would modify and approve the plan and bind the next president accordingly. In order to choose delegates, a national plebiscite was conducted in August with one delegate for every ten thousand so that each of the 170 electoral districts sent ten delegates. All of the delegates voted as a bloc for the presidential candidate favored in their district. The PNR spread its electoral machinery across the nation, turning the party's selection of delegates into an endorsement of the individual decided upon at the convention, the delegates essentially became national electors.

In 1933 Calles left the capital to spend the summer in Ensenada, Baja California, at President Rodríguez's luxurious El Sauzal compound. A steady flow of politicians made the trip to El Sauzal to confer with Calles in advance of the convention. Many names came up as possible presidential candidates, but soon the field was narrowed to three. An effort was made to ascertain whether each had sufficient support or too strong opposition to be viable. Emissaries shuttled around the republic checking with those considered the most politically knowledgeable. Significantly, rumors of military revolts did not disturb the nation. The culling of ambitious generals provides a partial explanation, as does the professionalizing of the army. Of even more importance, the political mood of the country had changed. Violence shifted to local clashes over candidates with regional implications perhaps, but not national ones. All interest groups appeared to be taken care of within the revolution, with the exception of the Church. The clergy, too weak to offer more than token protests over the idea of socialist education, still functioned as a foil for posturing radicals.

Calles had a northerner in mind for president, Gen. Manuel Pérez Treviño from Coahuila. Nevertheless two individuals besides Pérez Treviño made up the list, Sen. Carlos Riva Palacio and Gen. Lázaro Cárdenas. President Rodríguez left the politics—what he called "the political nuisance"—to Calles, while he administered the republic with his customary firmness. He pledged that his government would remain neutral, allowing the citizens (PNR, that is) to select the candidate freely. Calles's central role in the party made him the *gran elector*, but did not convey the ability to impose his choice on the convention. Agrarian delegates dominating the convention made land reform a central issue, brushing aside Calles's belief that it should be phased out or at the very least slowed down. Education and the Church issue resurfaced. The delegate from Tabasco, Arnulfo Pérez H., the self-proclaimed "personal enemy of God," demanded that the Church should be totally excluded from education and be replaced by "socialist education," a term that indicated different things to many, but basically called for student solidarity with the working class and a antireligious stance.[5] An expanded education program became a part of the six-year plan. The convention envisioned twelve thousand new rural schools. President Rodríguez suggested some new wording that the government would see to it that unions would not become oppressive. The delegates selected General Lázaro Cárdenas as the party's presidential candidate.

Suggested Reading

Balderrama, Francisco E., and Raymond Rodríguez. *Decade of Betrayal: Mexican Repatriation in the 1930s*. Albuquerque: University of New Mexico Press, 1995.

Bliss, Katherine Elaine. *Compromised Positions: Prostitution, Public Health, and Gender Politics in Revolutionary Mexico City*. University Park: Pennsylvania State University Press, 2001.

Tannenbaum, Frank. *Mexico: The Struggle for Peace and Bread*. New York: Alfred A. Knopf, 1962.

Vaughan, Mary Kay. *Politics in Revolution: Teachers, Peasants, and Schools, 1930–1940*. Tucson: University of Arizona Press, 1997.
Vaughan, Mary Kay, and Stephen Lewis. *The Eagle and the Virgin: Nation and Cultural Revolution, 1920–1940*. Durham NC: Duke University Press, 2006.

LÁZARO CÁRDENAS IN POWER 4

(*Previous page*) 4. Calendar girl. Calendars became the medium of images of revolutionary social types that circulated across the nation, especially in the 1930s. Calendar the property of Angela Villalba. Used with permission.

The Importance of Being a Revolucionario

General Lázaro Cárdenas had experienced a nearly perfect revolutionary career: he had joined the Madero Revolt, opposed Victoriano Huerta's seizure of power, and backed Carranza until Obregón issued his Plan of Agua Prieta. Subsequently he fought with Calles against de la Huerta, served as governor of his home state of Michoacán, and supported Calles as the first president of the PNR. For every revolutionary with a perfect record of being on the right side, at least five had made wrong choices. Among the many who made fatal missteps, Generals Arnulfo R. Goméz and Francisco R. Serrano stand out. Their revolt against Calles and the reelection of Obregón in 1927 lasted only briefly, ending in their deaths at the Huitzilac Massacre and at the graveyard in Coatepec. Lesser revolutionaries fled into exile in San Antonio, El Paso, and Los Angeles. A revolutionary establishment dominated politics and its members asserted their claim to high public office. Their male children inherited their mantles. Of all the veterans of revolutionary violence and survivors of politics who played with life-and-death stakes, Cárdenas had climbed to the top because of his commitment, astuteness, daring, and luck.

President Lázaro Cárdenas (1934–1940)

Once selected as the PNR's nominee, General Cárdenas set off on a campaign odyssey that covered eighteen thousand miles. The candidate visited villages that had never seen a state governor, let alone a national figure and the next president of the republic. Cárdenas left citizens amazed and delighted to be included in the election process. He used trains, planes, and cars, the latter traveling on roads built under President Calles, as well as even mules at times, going down almost imperceptible trails to reach tiny settlements. Such a trip would not have been possible a decade before. Even those who did not actually meet Cárdenas understood that he had reached out to citizens everywhere in the nation. His travels reported over the PNR's radio station XEFO reached voters across the country. Concluding his campaign, he made an election-eve radio address from Durango in which he discussed the six-year plan and his understanding of what had to be done. He declared that cooperatives had to become the revolution's ideal and announced plans for the construction of an expanded transportation grid of roads, rail, airways, and shipping routes. Overall he described a national economy directed by the federal administrators who would ensure a nonexploitive capitalism.

Cárdenas noted that foreign and private investors still had a place in the new economy as long as they respected the goals of the revolution and the laws of the country. Such statements broadcast to the entire nation reached the people in the same way as Franklin D. Roosevelt's "fireside chats" in the United States. Cárdenas created the feeling with listeners that he was in the room, speaking directly to them. He won the election as expected. Of more importance, he did so by a landslide of 2,225,000 votes, with the closest contender receiving only 24,395 votes. To the surprise of politicians flooding into Mexico City and anxious to sort out the fruits of victory, Cárdenas continued to tour the republic and listen to his constituents. As president he spent 489 days of his six-year term on the road, visiting 1,028 cities, towns, and villages. The combination of presidential visits and radio created a new political dynamism that led to a personal bond with citizens, a connection that many felt for the first time.

Cárdenas's tours drew crowds. No doubt many curious individuals came to see a presidential candidate for the first time, but Cárdenas worried that politics might wear thin and interest might wane. He wanted to insure continued excitement about his visit, so he traveled with mariachis. He was accompanied on some trips by the Mariachi Conculense of Cirilo Marmolejo and on others by the Mariachi Vargas de Tecalitlán. The original members of the Conculense group had made the first recordings of mariachi music in 1908. The group had played for the revolutionary governor of Jalisco and appeared at various Mexico City revolutionary gatherings organized by the director of public health, Luis Rodríguez Sánchez, from the same hometown. This mariachi band was the first to perform in a legitimate stage show at the Iris Theater and they appeared in the first Mexican sound movie, *Santa*. In 1933 the Mariachi Conculense visited Chicago to play at the World's Fair. Their style of dress—which included traditional sombreros with chin straps and hat bands, red ponchos over muslin pants and shirts, and red sashes around their waists—set the standard for all succeeding mariachi bands.

By traveling throughout the nation, the mariachis helped make the president's arrival memorable and simultaneously popularized their music and made it the national music. Mariachi Vargas, founded in 1898 by Gaspar Vargas in Jalisco, was under the direction of his son, Silvestre. They also toured with the president and played at his inauguration. Many residents in the capital still saw the mariachis as a novelty, although they were popular with revolutionary government officials from the west and north of the country. The Vargas group played with other mariachis at the capital city's popular Garibaldi Square and on the major radio station XEW, but still could not make enough money to stay in the capital. At this critical junction, Cárdenas used his influence to have the Vargas group named the official band of the city's police department and they continued in the position for the next twenty years. In 1937 the Vargas mariachi appeared in the *ranchera* movie *Así es mi Tierra* (*My Country Is Like This*), the first of their some two hundred films. During the same year the group made its first recordings for Peerless, the Mexican recording company, and in 1938 they signed with RCA Victor Mexicana and worked closely with artistic director Mariano Rivera Conde. During the 1930s mariachi music eventually surpassed even boleros as the most common music on radio and in movies, providing the soundtrack of the era. Mariachi Vargas, known as "the World's Greatest Mariachi," continues to perform today.

By traveling with mariachis during his presidential campaign, Cárdenas demonstrated the growing significance of cultural changes that had accompanied the revolution, the rise of radio, movies, comic books, and recorded music—all centered in the city. Mexicans appropriated what they saw and heard, and reshaped these to their liking. No better example of this exists than the adaptation of images from great murals on public buildings, which were altered to suit the appropriating artists and distributed as images on calendars.

The most evocative statements of people's romantic conceptions of the nation's past, its traditions revived by the revolutionaries, and dreams of the future came in these free calendars hanging on the walls of nearly every home. The artists, whose painted images were photographed for reproduction through photolithography, owed a debt of gratitude to Vasconcelos, who in the 1920s had sent photographers across the country to record the nation's ethnic and regional diversity. The calendar artists used their photos as inspiration just as they used murals. Of all the photographs none were more widely adapted than those by Luis Márquez, who documented rural Mexico in thousands of photos, some of which depicted 2,500 regionally distinctive women's dresses (*huipiles*) and other traditional clothing. Calendar artists flocked to rent his photographs as inspiration for their paintings. Without any of the international fanfare received by the muralists Diego Rivera, José Clemente Orozco, and Dávid Alfaro Siqueiros, calendar artists such as Jesús de la Helguerra, Antonio Gómez R., and Aurora Gil remained unrecognized but their work contributed to the formation of revolutionary national identity.[1]

The president-elect unbalanced the calculated distribution of power that Calles had so carefully crafted among the presidency, Congress, the PNR, and—through the party—workers and campesinos. Cárdenas used radicalism as a weapon against his revolutionary opponents and in the process strengthened the presidency. He took the oath of office in 1934 with Josephus Daniels, the U.S. ambassador, standing at his immediate left. In his inauguration address he declared that his travels throughout the republic had convinced him that Mexicans suffered from many injustices, from insufficient land to lack of employment opportunities. A divided labor movement, he said, had to confront capital while it engaged in destructive internal conflicts. Educators should identify with the proletariat and learn to work with the revolution. He called for a bureaucracy of dedicated civil servants, defining the standard of civil service simply as competence, and he made clear that he intended to demand competence from all government employees. Reminding government employees about whom they served, Cárdenas announced that he would devote an hour a day to hearing complaints or suggestions telegraphed to him at no cost.

Once Cárdenas assumed the presidency, he had to consolidate his authority. He appointed trusted generals to important political posts, choosing those who had been with him on the battlefield but who were not aligned with Calles. He also chose civilian experts to meet technical needs in the agricultural and financial ministries. Moreover he arranged to repeal the law that prevented the president from removing federal judges. In order to strengthen the judicial support of the programs he intended to pursue, he sent a list of judge nominees to Congress for approval. Some of these did not even have legal training, indicating the political nature of these appointments, but Congress approved them with without objection.

Cárdenas turned his attention to the army, which he determined to make subservient to his office. Newly minted junior officers, better educated and trained, began to infuse the old officer corps. The military school had admitted cadets from the lower classes and the army itself made a provision for promotion of capable individuals from the enlisted ranks. These personnel changed the face of the army. The president ordered all infantry officers to take examinations in military science. Those unable to pass the exams could take remedial training or retire. Rather than have the experience of schoolboys, many senior officers opted for retirement, made goodwill trips to foreign countries, or studied various subjects abroad at government expense.[2] Cárdenas divided the Ministry of War and Navy into two cabinet-level organizations, the Secretariat of National Defense and a separate Secretariat of the Navy.

The tone of the administration reflected Cárdenas's appreciation of the circumstances in which the lower classes lived. Rather than move into Chapultepec Castle, the traditional home of all presidents from the time of Juarez on, he moved into a common home built nearby, which he named after the place in Michoacán where he and his wife met. Today Los Pinos remains the official presidential residence. Aware of the puritanical streak among those excluded from what they imagined to be the morally loose life of politicians, the president ordered the closure of the stunning bar at the newly opened Palacio de Bellas Artes and shuttered popular casinos, including the Casino de la Selva. He ended legal gambling along the border, hoping to cut off an independent source of income for regional caciques, although it was the end of Prohibition in the United States that caused an immediate drop in revenues on the Mexican side of the border. Not everything could be so easily brought under control. Gen. Saturnillo Cedillo of San Luis Potosí proved too powerful to remove, so Cárdenas appointed him to the cabinet where he could be placed under constant observation.

Cárdenas's education minister, Ignacio García Téllez, declared that he intended to destroy the Church. A new law prohibited the post office from delivering religious materials. The government-sponsored Congress of the Proletarian Child sought to purge religion from everyday life, demanding that in schools the greeting "adios" be replaced by "salud." Programs of so-called of socialist education—coeducational, progressive, and scientific—would become nationalistic. The national government took charge of teacher training in order to ensure instruction in "social justice." In reality school attendance went down when socialist education became the prevailing doctrine, although few had any idea of what it meant in practice. Private schools also came under attack, as the president insisted that they teach socialist education or close. In Guadalajara eighty schools shut their doors, leading to riots. The governor finally declared a state of siege. Federal teachers who went too far against the Church faced hostile communities and—in some cases—assassination.

The administration also tackled the difficult task of incorporating indigenous peoples into the wider society. Cárdenas continued official support for the indigenous program in the Public Education Ministry. Moisés Sáenz and Carlos Basauri combined international and personal experience to shape the project. They built on Manuel Gamio's program of integrated development in the Teotihuacan Valley in the 1910s and the John Geinns Gray Memorial Expedition to Mexico in 1928 (jointly funded by Tulane University and the Ministry of Education), and added personal touches based on their own international travel and experience, to work on experimentation stations at Carapan, Michoacán, and Actopan, Hidalgo. Incorporating indigenous peoples resulted in new definitions of farmers and other rural residents. Rather than distinguishing between Indians and farm workers (called *labradores*), the revolutionaries referred to all country people regardless of ethnicity as campesinos (roughly, "peasants"). The term suggested the revolution's campaign to uplift the peasantry.

Cárdenas's radical rhetoric stirred labor to make demands. In 1933 only thirteen strikes had occurred, but the following year 202 strikes roiled urban centers, involving 14,685 workers, and in 1935 there were 642 strikes by some 145,212 workers. A strike against El Aguila Petroleum Company in early 1934 demanded five hundred thousand pesos in back pay for poor working conditions from the years 1906 to 1933. Significantly workers lumped the Porfirian and the revolution years together in their demands for social justice. Huasteca oil workers followed El Aguila employees out on strike. Puebla experienced a general strike followed by one in Veracruz where strikers cut electricity to the port. Railway and streetcar workers threatened to isolate Mexico City, on the heels of a taxi strike. Telephone workers and even movie theater attendants ran up red-and-black strike banners. In León strikers interrupted electricity, sanitation, and water service to the city's one hundred thousand inhabitants. Strikers affiliated with the CROM in some regions clashed violently with other unions.

The massive inconvenience caused by strikes had a social impact, but President Cárdenas remained unperturbed. Not so expresident Calles, who on his return from medical treatment in Los Angeles lashed out at labor unions and at divisiveness in Congress. In a statement published widely by the press in June 1935 ("Patriotic Declaration by General Plutarco Elías Calles"), he accused workers and congressmen of treason. The PNR newspaper, *El Nacional*, did not publish the statement. Whether Calles intended to confront Cárdenas or not remains unclear. As an exceptionally astute politician, Calles must have thought through the situation carefully. Cárdenas interpreted the statement's allusions to the days of President Ortiz Rubio as expressing Calles's hopes to reduce him to the same status. Labor unions rallied to Cárdenas's side, but Congress and the army wavered.

Moving quickly, Cárdenas dispatched emissaries to call on prominent politicians and military officers to determine their loyalty. The rapidity with which they had to respond meant that everyone pledged to support the president. Cárdenas drew up his own statement in which he pointed out that strikes, if settled fairly, strengthened the economy. At the same time, he noted that laws protected both sides and said that he would not permit excesses. Expressing full confidence in the patriotism and prudence of labor and peasant associations, Cárdenas skillfully forced a choice on the country between himself, the constitutional president, and the ex-president acting beyond his time. The widespread support for President Cárdenas pushed Calles to leave for Sinaloa, then to go into exile in Los Angeles, California.

Surprisingly, though, Calles returned to Mexico City in the middle of December 1935, ostensibly to defend his reputation. At the same time leftist students had taken over the National University. President Cárdenas prepared to confront what might become another crisis and directed that the newspapers refuse to publish statements by Calles. The former president started his own newspaper, *El Instante*, but it lasted only briefly. The potential crisis seemed to have arrived with the dynamiting of the

Veracruz–Mexico City passenger train. The unknown perpetrators escaped, but suspicion fell on Morones and Calles as those behind the outrage. Demonstrations and congressional committees demanded Calles's expulsion from the country or his arrest and trial. On April 10, 1936, presidential guards escorted Calles, Morones, and several of their close associates to the Mexico City airport, where they were placed aboard an airplane bound for Brownville, Texas (Calles carrying with him a copy of Hitler's *Mein Kampf*). Eventually Calles ended up back in Los Angeles stripped of any political authority.

Significantly the president and the former president battled in the arena of public opinion. Calles's initial victory was reversed as Cárdenas presented his rebuttal. It became clear that Mexicans in general supported the incumbent. Many worried about an army revolt, particularly after the dynamiting of the Veracruz–Mexico City train. It did not happen, partly as a result of Cárdenas's rapid action but more a consequence of military reforms. Cárdenas had also built a network of support through his campaign and visits across the country, and especially through the implementation of the revolutionary programs.

Cárdenas's Socioeconomic Program

Cárdenas intended to make good on promises that he had made during the election campaign, especially those expressed in the six-year plan. First he had a few housekeeping items that drew his attention. The president purged Calles supporters within the PNR. Then he turned to the problems of the countryside. Cárdenas believed that he understood rural people and their land hunger. His background provided a bond with those who lived and worked in rural villages. Born during the height of Porfirian prosperity in the small village of Jiquilpan, Michoacán, on his father's land, he endured the hardships of the countryside. The family property, once described dismissively as a bunch of rocks, nevertheless provided relative status amid impoverished villagers. With the help of one horse, the entire family worked to survive.

The president's trips throughout the rural parts of country made a deep impression on him. He believed that inadequate land and credit hampered the productivity of the peasantry but did not incapacitate them, as often asserted by commercial landholders. Unlike his predecessors, Cárdenas favored *ejidos* over individual ownership. Communal land grants incorporated entire communities, theoretically providing pooled labor and resources. Moreover large expanses of communal land duplicated the advantages of commercial agriculture's scale. The almost total lack of rural infrastructure—potable water, electricity, effective sanitation, schools—required that the resources of large *ejidos* be supplemented by government funds. The president's ideal *ejido* was the one established near Torreón. The Laguna cotton *ejido,* created in 1937 of over a million acres, included schools, a hospital in Torreón, cooperative mills, and modern machinery. The Laguna *ejido* had the advantage of existing modern infrastructure and a steady market for cotton.

In spite of Calles's road-building program, many villages remained isolated outposts, remote from authority and scarcely part of the regional economy. Lack of storage facilities forced the immediate sale of crops at a low price. Breaking down the isolation and allowing small producers to store their harvests and wait for a better prices, Cárdenas continued the road-building program and created the Almacenes Nacionales de Depósito, S. A. (ANDSA) in 1936. Within a year it had 177 warehouses, with a combined holding capacity of 160,000 tons. A certificate of deposit from ANDSA could be used as collateral for purchases.

The amount of land redistributed under President Cárdenas far exceeded the amount distributed by other revolutionary presidents. One-third to one-half of the rural population had received land by the end of his term, as approximately forty-five million acres of the existing cropland was transferred, including the return of land lost during the Porfiriato by the Yaqui Indians. It represented the apex of land reform that would never again be matched. The breadth of this program gave it success, but agrarian problems and poverty remained. As the members of *ejidos* reverted to subsistence agriculture, the decline of food production for the market threatened shortages in the growing cities. Government assistance, from furnishing seed and machinery to credit and agricultural expertise, fell short of needs. Demographic pressures soon pinched the land resources and encouraged migration into cities.

Public health formed a major effort of the social revolution, especially during the Cárdenas presidency. Health officials initiated health campaigns directed against prostitution, contagious diseases, and poor physical fitness. Prohibiting prostitution, vaccinating citizens against yellow fever and other communicable diseases, and fostering sports and exercise programs in the schools and in the military all served to promote general health. The schools also gave lessons in hygiene and cleanliness to encourage general well-being.

The good life brought to every village by radio had an impact on the younger generation anxious not to repeat the grinding life of their parents. Official party propaganda trumpeted new material advances, particularly in the capital. Movies indicated the possibility of another lifestyle, even when Hollywood portrayed Mexicans in negative stereotypes. Urbanization made farmers into workers in the modern sense, with different political perceptions and daily concerns that had to be addressed.

The political and economic future lay with workers, factories, and concentrated capital. The revolutionaries had reached the point where they recognized that they had limited good land to redistribute and that they needed to devise new programs to achieve social justice. As veterans the revolutionaries had relied on their battlefield experience and occasionally on the advice of civilian advisers. The revolutionary leadership had the urgent need to deal with an ever-more-complex national administration, to rationalize the ad hoc actions of the early days, and to structure a maze of uncoordinated agencies. Moreover the sons and daughters of revolutionaries born after the fall of Díaz in 1911 had a different perception of the nation's past and a preoccupation with its future.

The need for more educated officials relegated many generals to senior political positions. The task of setting broad policy remained in their hands but implementation relied on an educated generation, one trained in the autonomous enclave of the National University and universities abroad. Civilians able to deal with complicated financial and economic problems as well as vexing social concerns—including primary education, indigenous issues, public health, and road building—already occupied the secondary levels of government. Sub-secretary of

Foreign Relations Ramón Beteta represented the new generation. He worked for Gen. Eduardo Hay, the secretary of foreign affairs and an important political appointee. Nevertheless President Cárdenas relied more on Beteta, the son of a lawyer father and a mother from a wealthy, landed family. Beteta had graduated from the University of Texas in 1923 with a BA in economics, achieved a law degree from the National University (UNAM), and then received the first UNAM PhD in social science. Beteta formed part of Cárdenas's "brain trust."[3]

Uniting the new generation under the revolution's banner required the fabrication and acceptance of a revolutionary myth, a task that could only be done by intellectuals able to distill the essence of events and flesh out underlying intentions. They boiled down sophisticated interpretations to the point of propaganda to use in schools and during rallies. The powerful symbols they created provided the social glue that bound together individuals with a shared sense of nationalism. The importance of intellectuals, with deep roots in Hispanic culture, took on well-understood political functions as they shaped the myth of the revolution.

The CROM's influence followed the fate of its leader, Luis Morones, whom Cárdenas forced into exile in New York City. Vicente Lombardo Toledano had little difficulty displacing the CROM with his Confederación de Trabajadores Mexicanos (CTM). Cárdenas favored Lombardo Toledano, appointing him minister of labor. Given the objective of raising the minimum-wage level to four pesos a day from the 1.6 peso daily average, Toledano failed. Unfortunately prices increased to keep nominal wages at the previous low level. Cárdenas then approved strikes, and when companies complained that they could not earn a profit he advised them to turn over their factories to the workers or to the government. He also began to experiment with government factories such as a sugar refinery in Morelos and he nationalized ownerships of the railways. He also favored the consolidation of petroleum unions. The first National Petroleum Conference in 1935 led to the creation of the Sindicato de Trabajadores Petroleros de la Republica Mexicana (STPRM) the next year, eventually with over thirteen thousand members.

Manufacturing interests posed somewhat of a dilemma. It could not be argued that factories had been taken away from the people as land had clearly been. Nevertheless wages, working conditions, and prices became issues of concern to the national regime when they were perceived as being exploitive. Monterrey industrialists became the center of business resistance to Cárdenas. Shaken by what they saw as growing radicalism under Cárdenas and the Soviet rhetoric used by Lombardo Toledano and the CTM, they prepared to battle the federal government. The Monterrey Rotary Club became one of the bastions of resistance. Luis G. Sada and Roberto G. Sada, part of the family that organized the Monterrey Group, led the response. Educated at the Massachusetts Institute of Technology and the University of Michigan respectively, they had cross-border ties, not the least of which were through the Rotarians. These industrial leaders were connected to mid-sized entrepreneurs and smaller businessmen through the Monterrey Chamber of Commerce. Manuel Barragán, who served a term as president of the Chamber of Commerce, managed the local Coca-Cola bottling plant and directed the magazine *Actividad* that glorified the accomplishments and contributions of business. They cemented alliances with revolutionary veterans anxious to get rich through business investments.

General Aarón Sáenz, former governor of Nuevo León, who had praised the entrepreneurial effort of the Monterrey Group, appeared to be the ideal revolutionary businessman. He had become Obregón's chief of staff as a young man. Subsequently he served as President Ortiz Rubio's secretary of education. Later as the secretary of industry, commerce, and labor in the same administration, he drew up the 1931 Federal Labor Act the same year that Mexico joined the International Labor Organization (ILO). Under President Rodríguez, Sáenz directed the Federal District, a post that he held into the early years of the Cárdenas regime. As a Calles supporter, he prudently resigned after the break between the two men. An admiring book about General Sáenz referred to him as Mexico's "revolutionary capitalist."[4]

Cárdenas's programs for workers upset the balance in Monterrey and Nuevo León. The growing power of the federal government evened out the diverse programs that made the revolution different across the various states. Mexico City increasingly dictated the political reaction in Nuevo León and elsewhere. The new balance of power now threatened industrialists and their favorable accommodation with state government officials.

The Cárdenas regime intended to enforce the labor code of 1931 and favor labor's demands. In Monterrey the Cuauhtémoc brewery and its glass factory became symbolic targets, but all industrial groups came under union pressure. As a major step toward shifting power to the CTM, in 1936 a labor arbitration board declared company unions illegal. The Confederación Patronal de la República Mexicano (COPARMEX), organized by business interests, sprang to the offensive. Borrowing the general-strike tactic from labor, employers conducted a citywide lockout accompanied by demonstrations that completely closed the industrial city down. Speeches recast the struggle as one between "Mexicanism and Communism." They alleged that President Cárdenas and Vicente Lombardo Toledano undermined family values and functioned as ideological agents of Moscow. Conservative groups rallied to the cause. A state of civic rebellion led to violence. Acción Cívica, the most aggressive antigovernment group, came under gunfire and a hail of rocks, as workers attempted to break up the organization's meeting. The police arrested six hundred attendees, holding then in jail overnight, in an unsuccessful effort to break the group.

In the 1930s the national government grappled with an unexpected problem. The sudden decline of the U.S. economy following the Wall Street debacle of 1929 rapidly turned into an economic collapse and a social disaster. Laid-off workers strained relief resources to the breaking point. Mexicans who had moved north, drawn by the opportunities of the Roaring Twenties, swelled the ranks of the unemployed throughout the United States. County welfare bureaucracies responded with repatriation schemes to deal with unneeded foreign workers and avoid welfare costs. Repatriation resulted from local and county programs and money rather than state or federal initiatives. While other indigent foreigners also left the United States, Mexican laborers made up a significant proportion of those repatriated. Often unskilled, they were some of the first to be laid off and became dependent on welfare for survival. Repatriation on a much smaller scale had been used in the brief economic downturn that followed the end of the world war. Now as then it took several forms, voluntary, by intimidation, and through deportation. Many agreed to leave, fearing that harsher measures would be employed if they remained.

By ship (from California and New York), train, truck, bus, and car, Mexicans made their way to the border and an uncertain future in Mexico. They came from New York, New Orleans, Los Angeles, Tucson, Detroit, Chicago, Pittsburgh, Kansas City, Norfolk, and even Fairbanks, Alaska, among other places.[5] Mexican consulates did their best to help, although they had only limited funds. The consulate in Los Angeles provided information on colonization schemes under consideration by the government and attempted to help as much as possible. Many officials advised families to stay put and wait for economic conditions to improve. This option required that they avoid welfare and use their own assets to ride out the Depression. The lack of coordination made suffering inevitable. U.S. authorities believed that their job ended when the repatriated had been placed on designated transportation out of the county. A Los Angeles county commissioner calculated that the repatriation program saved the county $435,000. Train travel to the border could take a week or more from the Midwest under miserable conditions. Babies and the elderly suffered, at times even died. Penetrating the interior of Mexico also presented major difficulties. In spite of road building in the 1920s and the availability of railroads, entry points did not permit easy access to many secondary cities and towns, let alone isolated villages. Border cities struggled with massively increased populations.

Officials, commentators, and ordinary Mexicans responded

ambivalently toward the returnees. Some officials asserted that those who came back had useful skills that they could teach others and that they would help the nation become more productive. The National Repatriation Committee (NRC) turned to government agencies, businesses, and charities to deal with the problem. The lack of success led President Rodríguez to replace the committee with the National Repatriation Board in July 1934. Congressman Gilberto Fabila denied that the revolutionary government had any responsibility, because preceding governments had allowed the transborder migration to occur. Others worried that returnees might introduce political instability, leading to a social uprising as a consequence of ideas picked up in the United States or from past conflicts such as those of the Cristeros who had fled across the border.

In reality the cultural differences may have been more important than current or past political ideas. Children, often U.S. citizens, spoke English among themselves, preferred expensive flour tortillas, played baseball, and dressed as the gringos they had become. One returnee, Emilia Castañeda de Valenciana, proudly recalled that they did not fit in and she eventually returned to her native Los Angeles as World War II opened up jobs again. Custom officials noted that under the *franquicias* (customs exemptions), returnees brought in an amazing array of items unavailable to their compatriots. Businessmen suspected smuggling and resented what they saw as competition. Government statistics record some 415,000 returnees. How many later went back to the United States is unknown, but the number is believed to have been substantial. The repatriation demonstrated that relations between the two counties had broadened beyond political and economic matters to social issues and questions of nationality and responsibility.[6]

Suggested Reading

Bantjes, Adrian. *As If Jesus Walked on Earth: Cardenismo, Sonora, and the Mexican Revolution*. Wilmington DE: SR Books, 1998.

Brading, David A., ed. *Caudillo and Peasant in the Mexican Revolution*. Cambridge MA: Cambridge University Press, 1980.

González, Luis. *San Jose de Gracia: Mexican Village in Transition*. Austin: University of Texas Press, 1982.

Knight, Alan. "Cardenismo: Juggernaut or Jalopy?" *Journal of Latin American Studies* 26, no. 1 (February 1994): 73–107.

Lieuwen, Edwin. *Mexican Militarism: The Political Rise and Fall of the Revolutionary Army, 1910–1940*. Albuquerque: University of New Mexico Press, 1968.

Villalba, Angela. *Mexican Calendar Girls/Chicas de Calendarios Mexicanos*. San Francisco: Chronicle Books, 2006.

5

THE TIPPING POINT

(*Previous page*) 5. Drawing by school child. The Secretariat of Public Education sponsored a number of pro-grams to encourage children to draw pictures or write stories about their society. This picture represents an urban child's image of luxury, a Popsicle. Image from the personal collection of Elena J. Albarrán. Used with permission.

An international financial crisis suddenly arrived again in the spring of 1937. A world depression that year forced national leaders to seek accommodation as they faced a financial collapse and could not afford to battle with industrialists. The cost of living index leapt into uncharted territory, with the sharpest rise in the twentieth century. Between 1934 and 1938 the cost of living jumped by some 53 percent. Wages fell far behind inflation in spite of past gains. Food supplies fell to dangerously low levels that threatened the urban population. This time the cause appeared to be falling productivity resulting in part from the land redistribution. Bean and corn production dropped off in 1935 and then leveled until 1938. Wheat production dropped 22 percent in 1937. Rising prices in the cities foreshadowed political problems with the growing urban population. In the 1930s Monterrey grew by 40 percent, Mexico City by 30 percent and Guadalajara by 27 percent, with no end of growth in sight.

Cárdenas responded with an effort to prevent activities by speculators and brokers. The state of Durango made private storage of basic grains illegal in an attempt to stop merchants and others from holding back supplies and raising prices. Other state officials did the same. In June 1937, the president created the Comité Regulador del Mercado de Trigo (CRMT) charged with the domestic and foreign purchase, storage, and sale of wheat.[1] The CRMT included producer representatives as well as bureaucrats.

Late in the year the organization imported some five thousand tons to cover the shortfall in production. Following a technical group's recommendation, the president replaced the CRMT with another agency charged with balancing the market for all foodstuffs, from corn and beans to wheat. The Comité Regulador del Mercado de las Subsistencias (CRMS), significantly, excluded producers. Established to deal with high prices and shortages, it set a minimum price for corn, beans, wheat, and rice, and made the national government the buyer of last resort. The agency attempted to keep prices at the level that assured a reasonable return to the producer. Those close to railway lines could take advantage of price supports, while small producers without all-weather roads remained at the mercy of local buyers. Freight charges favored large producers able to fill entire boxcars. A boxcar shortage made it even more difficult for small shippers to reserve space. The government did not want to admit that urban supply considerations gave aid to cities priority over aid to small farmers.

The government set retail prices based upon recommendations of a committee headed by the governors of each state, with broad membership that included consumers. The ANDSA, pushed by the CTM, entered the retail market, selling to merchants who then sold to the public at fixed prices. By the end of 1938, twenty-five ANDSA stores had opened in the capital. The agency also helped unions open stores for their members and encouraged other groups to establish cooperatives. Consumers in Mexico City benefited more than those in other parts of the nation. Pressure to address high prices mounted in the last three years of the administration, as real wages declined. Nevertheless the price of bread and corn went up, though at a lower rate than other staples. The flurry of activity to provide price relief, as well as attacks on brokers and speculators, obscured Cárdenas's retreat from land distribution. Subsidizing food prices, importing cereals from the United States, and increasing production by providing seed, insecticides, and expertise to commercial interests, required cutting funding for other programs. Further cuts loomed, as the peso lost value and the financial system teetered on the verge of collapse. The recognition that the revolution's primary constituency had changed from peasants to workers and from villages to the cities had far ranging consequences.

Credit markets contracted as strikes against the petroleum industry led to the flight of capital out of the country. An empty treasury threatened to shut down the country. Treasury Minister Eduardo Suárez moved boldly, issuing bonds backed by the cotton and sugar harvest as collateral. He used the reserves of the Bank of Mexico to float additional bonds and negotiated loans to keep public-works projects going. A 3 percent income tax and corporate tax completed the immediate rescue, but the long-term financial outlook remained grim. In the United States President Roosevelt continued to buy silver as before and to preserve the peso exchange rate arranged for the U.S. treasury he made a one-time purchase of thirty-five million pesos of Mexican gold. This saved the economy but barely so. The year ended with a deficit of 120 million pesos, making the financing of social programs difficult and in some cases impossible.

In the midst of these domestic concerns, international issues intruded into daily life. The Spanish Civil War appeared to be the beginning of a world war between fascism and the Left, including communism and liberal democracy. Many worried that the civil war in Spain provided a glimpse of what might happen in Mexico. Conservative groups, already convinced that Cárdenas intended to push the country toward communism, admired Spain's Gen. Francisco Franco as the personification of the Hispanic tradition of family and religion. The Gold Shirts, a right-wing group that emerged in Mexico City, reflected Franco's programs and suggested that fascism had begun to appeal to some conservatives. It never gained ground during the Cárdenas regime but a larger and more popular group took its place in the 1940s. With the rise of Italian and German fascism, good relations with the United States became crucial—an objective jeopardized by the petroleum crisis.

The oil industry had long been plagued with labor unrest, but in May 1937 some seventeen thousand workers walked off the job, demanding higher wages, better housing, schools, and medical services. Unable to arrive at an agreement, the workers and industry went to arbitration. The results favored the workers so the companies appealed to the Supreme Court, but by that time the strike had become a national issue and the court ruled against the companies. Rather than accepting this, the U.S. and British companies refused to comply with the ruling. Their decision risked transforming the strike into a matter of national sovereignty. British oil companies, with much more at stake, leaned toward giving in to the wage demands, but did not act, convinced by their U.S. colleagues that Washington would force the Mexican government to back down. In fact a divided U.S. government, split between State Department support for the oil companies and Secretary of the Treasury Henry Morgenthau's distaste for economic coercion, needed time to develop an official approach.

Caught between damaging the court's jurisdiction and his own authority or confronting Washington and London by upholding the law, President Cárdenas decided on a courageous course. On March 18, 1938, under the provisions of Article 123 of the Constitution of 1917, he announced over the radio that the oil industry had been nationalized. Cárdenas, who had lost most of his popularity as a result of the crisis of 1937, now became a national hero.

Oil companies attacked Cárdenas and his government as a gang of Bolsheviks and bandits who had held them up and robbed them. Both houses of the U.S. Congress passed a resolution in support of military intervention. Public opinion in United States did not support the use of force, nor did the president, who ignored the call for war. The issue became a question of compensation. Roosevelt reminded the public that Cárdenas had promised to compensate the companies. Roosevelt also directed Secretary of Treasury Morgenthau to continue the purchase of silver to protect the value of the peso. Ambassador Josephus Daniels expressed strong preference for moving to an agreement to compensate oil companies for expropriated property, but otherwise he refused to support the oil companies. He used his personal connection with the U.S. president to block the State Department's heavy-handed attempts to intimidate Cárdenas and stop the purchase of silver.

By that time the battle had come down to one of accountants. Ambassador Daniels played a central role in keeping compensation demands realistic. Oil companies came up with a value of

$450 million. Eventually Mexico paid $130 million. Meanwhile the companies withheld parts and equipment, oil tankers, and expertise, believing that Mexicans could not run the industry. In fact the government had some experience with oil through its national company, Petróleos Nacionales de Mexico (PETROMEX). In January 1937 Cárdenas transformed PETROMEX into the Administración General del Petróleo Nacional (AGPN), a government-owned company that produced 3.79 percent of the country's oil.

Nevertheless the government's inexperience in the international market could not be denied. Attempts to close markets for Mexican oil failed as Germany and Italy took up much of the production. With production recovered to previous levels by 1940, Cárdenas formed a federal corporation, Petróleos Mexicanos (PEMEX), to run the properties. In one effort to soften U.S. public opinion PEMEX started a travel club in 1940 and began publication in English of the PEMEX travel club bulletin mailed without cost to interested readers. Articles, often written by U.S. citizens living in Mexico, described the country's culture and history for the curious tourist. A listing of monthly events, description of road conditions, and an offer to mail complete information on motoring in Mexico represented an early effort to develop mass tourism, but at the time the objective to foster understanding was more important than revenue.

The overwhelming national support for expropriation of the oil companies extended to Church leaders. Their support for the expropriation led to a conciliatory period in relations between Cárdenas and the hierarchy. In 1938 Pope Pius XI authorized the celebration in Mexico of the Holy Year of Jubilee. This represented the first time that it had been held in the

Western Hemisphere. The celebration ran from October 12, the day commemorating the arrival of Christianity in the Western Hemisphere—and the crowning of the Virgin of Guadalupe in 1895, to the end of the year. A brief return to hostility would occur in December 1939 when Congress would pass the Socialist Education Act to amend Article 3 of the 1917 Constitution. An angry hierarchy would throw its political support to an opposition candidate in the upcoming election.

Subsequently in 1938, taking advantages of a surge in his popularity as well strident expressions of nationalism that followed the oil expropriation, Cárdenas ordered the PNR to abolished itself and reemerge as the Mexican Revolutionary Party (PRM). The new party had well-defined corporate sections representing labor (Confederación de Trabajadores Mexicanos—CTM), peasants (Confederación Nacional de Campesinos—CNC), the military, and civil servants (Confederación Nacional de Obreros Públicos—CNOP). This corporate organization provided greater control of the party by the leadership.

Overlooked in the heat of the moment, the Cárdenas administration had changed the nature of its revolutionary experiment. The president recognized that revolutionary programs to redistribute the nation's wealth could not meet the needs of the people. A growing population and burgeoning urbanization overwhelmed redistribution programs. Ironically Cárdenas had arrived at the same conclusion that had motivated Calles to increase electrical power and attract automobile assembly plants, such as the one opened by Ford in 1925. In 1933 Calles had established the Nacional Financiera as a government-funded industrial-development institution. With the blessing of President

Cárdenas, the Financiera together with the Bank of Mexico, aided by the expertise of economists Eduardo Suárez and Eduardo Villaseñor, reoriented the underlying direction of the revolution. At this point nationalism replaced revolutionary promises, and the stamp "Hecho en Mexico" (Made in Mexico) dulled the pain of monopoly prices and often-shoddy products.

The impending world war required a reexamination of the domestic situation and relations with the United States. Ambassador Josephus Daniels had been supportive of the revolution and obviously respected the government leaders. He laid some of the groundwork for a more positive turn in relations between the two countries. Daniels, portrayed in the United States as a "benevolent geezer" who accepted whatever the Mexican government told him, and thought of by his supporters as a "wise old owl," became extremely popular in Mexico City. He matched Dwight Morrow as one of the most popular U.S. ambassadors in the twentieth century. He tended to see both Cárdenas's actions and Roosevelt's programs in the United States as socially necessary and proper.

Internally Cárdenas feared that the radical Right and communist Left, now bound together as a result of the Soviet-Nazi pact, might be able to mount an armed rebellion on the eve of the 1940 presidential election. Such an event might provoke U.S. intervention with the result that the country might be reduced to being a pawn in a larger game. Roosevelt had concerns about rumors of Nazi spies and sympathizers in Mexico, and he wanted close cooperation to deal with the threat. He also sought approval for U.S. military air reconnaissance over areas where enemies might establish a beachhead. Given all these factors,

Roosevelt suggested a bilateral defense agreement with provisions that could lead to U.S. intervention under certain circumstances, but Cárdenas refused the suggestion. To shore up defensive forces, he ordered the army to incorporated all federal police forces and subsequently customs officials. In May 1940 national military conscription became law. The army, unlike Cárdenas, favored bilateral cooperation to receive training in combat operations and to obtain weapons from the United States. Some army officers envisioned a victorious United States emerged from the war as an imperialist threat and armed with the latest weapons. High officials thus cast the United States in a protective role on one hand and on the other as a predatory wolf.

The mixed motivation with which officials approached Washington on the eve of World War II obscured their eagerness to take an expanded role in international politics. While suspicions remained on military issues, economists saw opportunity. Minister of the Treasury Suárez recognized that wartime demand for raw materials would be a bonanza for the country. Integration of the economy into the wartime raw-material supply chain had financial and technical advantages. It also meant that internal industrial development could be accelerated. Industrial interest in Monterrey and elsewhere would not be politically unbalanced or economically challenged in the interest of labor. Moreover demand for workers could be expected to rise along with wages. Commercial agriculture came back into favor because of its export potential.

Much depended on the right man to succeed President Cárdenas. The conservative wing of the PRM favored a man able to accommodate industrialists and businessmen. Of course that individual would still have to be a revolutionary, but from the Right. Manuel Avila Camacho had both the political and the revolutionary qualifications, though in regard to the latter some pundits called him "the unknown soldier." He had served as Carranza's paymaster for the Third Division in 1918 and subsequently, after the battle of Morelia in 1924, Obregón promoted him to general. He fought against the Cristeros and developed a close friendship with Cárdenas. Avila Camacho did not live the flashy life of many revolutionary generals—including his outrageous brother, Maximino—and many thought that he lacked charisma. His critics described him as boring and as being both physically and mentally heavy. The person who mattered most, though, President Cárdenas, agreed that he should be the candidate.

The Monterrey industrialists, unsure of what Cárdenas intended, decided to put up their own candidate and they chose Gen. Juan Almazán. A big man with a wonderful smile, he appeared to have to have popular support, at least in the capital. Present Cárdenas promised an honest election but journalists charged that he did not keep his word.

As expected, the official party's candidate won but backers of Almazán did not intend to accept the results. Even before the election contact with U.S. citizens interested in a more conservative Mexico—and possibly restoration of expropriated property—raised the question of a revolt. After the presidential election Almazán left for Cuba to assess his future. From a safe distance he could gauge international support and most importantly that of the U.S. government. Questioning the legitimacy of the election of Avila Camacho made it possible to claim to have been cheated out of the presidency. Major Mexico City newspapers announced the election results in advance of the official tally, raising some questions. Reportedly Cárdenas wavered about the results, but in the end he stuck with Avila Camacho. The official results gave the PRM candidate 2,476,641 votes to just 151,101 votes for Almazán. Few believed the tally, though, and both sides claimed victory. On September 1, 1940, supporters of Almazán met in the capital and appointed Gen. Héctor F. López provisional president until their candidate would take office in December. It remains unclear what Almazán's followers expected might come of this challenge. Cárdenas and his administration largely ignored their efforts.

An armed revolt remained the only option. Gen. Francisco Franco's regime in Spain appeared willing to help. Much depended on the reaction in Washington. Unknown to Almazán's supporters, a decision had already been made to support the PRM. Avila Camacho's selection as the party's candidate had received the prior approval of the U.S. State Department, with the condition that the Mexican government would not oppose U.S. military bases if needed and that it would favor military agreements and a commercial treaty.[2] President Roosevelt saw little to be gained by destabilizing the government in favor of Almazán. Not surprisingly, without Washington's assistance a plan to acquire arms to stage an effective seizure of the government ran into a maze of broken promises and logistical problems. The president's son Elliott Roosevelt became involved, providing a momentary burst of optimism. The planned uprisings fizzled as federal troops easily extinguished them. In Chilpancingo, Guerrero, Cárdenas dispatched two hundred Spanish Republican veterans along with airmen and planes to counter an expected attack.[3] Almazán's support among businessmen evaporated after it became obvious that Avila Camacho shared many of their objectives.

In another political move, Manuel Gómez Morín and others officially established the Partido Acción Nacional (PAN) on March 1, 1940, at the time written off as a conservative, Catholic, business party. In reality, Gómez Morín and the leadership presented a more academic, polished alternative to the official party. Nevertheless the PAN's ideological foundations rested on the 1927 manifesto of René Capistrán Garza, appointed the head of Catholic armies by the National League for the Defense of Religious Liberty. Capistrán Garza called for separation of church and state, political liberties, workers' rights, freedom of association, protection of capital, respect for private property, creation of a yeoman class of small property holders, and a fair distribution of land.[4] The PAN registered as an opposition party without any immediate hope of overturning the PRM. Its strength lay in the future, as the country urbanized and became more complex and sophisticated. Meanwhile, the PRM could not be denied.

Gen. Avila Camacho had earlier attempted to calm the Church's reaction to the socialist education legislation that he supported. At a public meeting in Guadalajara he declared his support for religious liberty and advised that the Church's harsh stand against socialist education represented an unnecessary overreaction. This represented Avila Camacho's first public indication of his conciliatory attitude toward the Church. When subsequently asked by an interviewer for the magazine *Hoy* about the pressing issues of the day, President Avila Camacho unambiguously reassured readers of his keen interest in national unity. On the Church question, he responded with a cryptic but reassuring comment: "I am a believer." As for labor, he declared his intension to govern in the interests of all Mexicans, an indication that labor could not expect special privileges. To the campesinos he expressed grave reservations about the future of *ejidos* and his preference for individual ownership. A series of measures to help entrepreneurs sealed the pragmatic accommodation. Already a successful businessman, Almazán returned to Mexico to add to his fortune, putting presidential ambitions aside.

As president, Avila Camacho served as the spokesman of the revolutionary generation and asserted its achievements. In October 1941, in an address to the Chamber of Deputies, he claimed, "We have the satisfaction of knowing that the Mexican Revolution is the first of the social movements of this century which has been fulfilled." He went on to elaborate that "the entire republic now demands material and spiritual conquest in a prosperous and powerful economy."[5]

Avila Camacho intended to curb union power in the interest of necessary industrial development in the face of the impending war. The CTM gathered strength under Cárdenas, while the CROM and other secondary national federations lost members and support. Avila Camacho did not intended to create one union federation for his labor support, but to reduce the multiple organizations to being cooperative instruments of government policy. A badly shaken Vicente Lombardo Toledano relinquished his leadership of the CTM and tried to reach an accommodation with the president. Curiously they had been childhood friends. Lombardo Toledano's wealthy background (copper) and Avila Camacho's lower-class family (muleteers) switched ideological roles and—as it turned out—destinies. The CTM selected Fidel Velázquez who had fought with Zapata as Avila Camacho's replacement.

Velázquez, although an economic conservative, made use of the Zapata myth to befriend workers. Under his control the CTM became a large bureaucratic union more responsive to the national regime than its membership. As disappointed affiliates withdrew, its revenues declined and the government stepped in to cover the shortfall. By 1950 62.2% of the CTM's monthly receipts came from the government. Nevertheless Avila Camacho saw to it that the CROM and other federated unions became administrative clients in varying degrees. The Pan American Confederation of Labor, supported by the American Federation of Labor (AFL), became the model preferred by the president but not by the workers.[6] Modifications to the federal labor law in 1942 set down the procedures that unions had to follow prior to a strike. An illegal strike carried penalties and risked destruction of the offending organization. Whether a strike met the proper legal qualifications became a political decision, one decided well before strikers took to the streets.[7]

Urbanization not only required better food distribution and more production, but new social institutions. A social security program was proposed, like the one introduced in the United States in 1933, to respond to the problem of an aging sector no longer able to depend on an extended family and farm work. Cárdenas had discussed the possibility during his administration, but dropped it as a consequence of the oil expropriation crisis. Unions favored the program on the whole, although some feared that industrialists might seize the opportunity to eliminate contractual benefits. Nevertheless the need remained acute, particularly in the capital city. President Avila Camacho—anxious to dispel the public view that he thought only of businessmen and profitable production—favored the idea. Without a single vote against it, the legislation passed both houses of Congress in 1943, creating the Instituto Mexicano de Seguro Social (IMSS). A commission representing the government, employees, and employers supervised the IMSS. The funds were provided by an employer contribution of 6 percent of a worker's salary, coupled with 3 percent of the salary contributed by the government and another 3 percent by the employee. Half of the fund went for medical care and half for pensions and disability insurance. Only industrial workers in the Federal District initially received coverage. The IMSS gained control over an expanding amount of money. The next year Monterrey and Puebla became eligible and Guadalajara workers became eligible for the plan in 1946. Not all workers were covered by the IMSS. Microenterprises and other parts of the informal economy, often the entry-level employment for newly arrived rural migrants, remained outside the social security safety net. The dispensing of medical services through the IMSS strengthened ties between privileged organized workers and the regime.[8]

President Avila Camacho attempted to duplicate on the national level Puebla's populist machine politics that had elevated him to the presidency. He used a full array of communication technology, but especially radio, to indoctrinate the public. With nationalism heightened by war concerns, radio was used to rally the nation and foster pride. Meanwhile contributions to Allied war efforts and the experience of being a respected part of the larger world opened people in both Mexico and the United States to cultural changes.

The new urban life, sophisticated night clubs, orchestras, youth-oriented entertainment, and modern fashions all overturned village traditions that had changed slowly in the past because of poverty and isolation. Singers—including Agustín Lara, Toña la Negra, and Jorge Negrete—sang lyrics that spoke to new situations and often jumped the border, becoming popular in the United States. "Besame Mucho" and "Diez Minutos Más" offended the older generation bewildered by the changes and apparently powerless to turn back the clock. Ranchero music linked the newly urbanized to their villages as well as updated their laments to the pitfalls of romantic love in urban settings. The frustrations of city life could be defused by widely popular movie-comedian Cantinflas and his various comic characterizations. His role as the *pelado* (streetwise vagrant) in the city alternated with those of the sleazy politician, union boss, and fat, bourgeoisie capitalist. These simplified comic characters represented the types that rural migrants encountered in city. They legitimated the migrants' confusion and judgment about city slickers and authorities they did not understand. Conversely the upper classes could laugh at themselves as they interacted with *pelados*. Significantly Cantinflas's comic movie in 1940, *Ahí Está el Detalle* (*That's the Point*) took on judicial authorities—lawyers and judges—an occupation group that migrants hoped to avoid. His popularity among all classes faded only when the times changed and real life overwhelmed even the comic.[9]

Women during the war years moved more directly into the public eye and a debate emerged over their role in society. The women's pages of the popular illustrated magazine *Hoy* focused on women's use of cosmetics and other beauty products. An article in 1946 reviewed the practice and concluded that modern women had an obligation to maintain their beauty, not out of vanity, but as a weapon more powerful than a vote in the struggle for their social advancement. The author identified makeup, perfume, and jewelry as women's most powerful weapons, but recognized the challenge for them of working like a man outside the home for eight hours, rushing home to cook, clean, and iron, and trying to look beautiful.

Feminist writers identified the changing roles of middle-class women and the redefinition of femininity in the 1940s, with the shifting boundaries of cultural behavior. Ignoring the traditional segregation of male and female space, activists of the fledgling feminist movement promoted various causes, such as women's suffrage (something that would not be realized until 1953). Taking a different approach to promote women's entry into the wage economy, the modern version of home economics called for the adoption of modern, laborsaving devices, such as electric irons and automatic washers, to replace more time-consuming practices.

The antifeminist argument emerged at the same time and charged that the new feminist behavior and platform for change represented masculine characteristics. Conservative social commentators abhorred women's new fashion trends that abandoned traditional bright colors and feminine ruffles in favor of straight lines, muted colors, and—worst of all—the wearing of trousers.

Many of them argued that the feminist movement would destroy femininity and feminine beauty.

The opposing writers often placed their debate within the framework of revolutionary nationalism or wartime cosmopolitanism, drawn chiefly from the United States. Newspapers and magazines displayed photographs of women engaged in work in wartime industries—building planes, ships, tanks, and guns—photos that came from the United States. They also reported on women's participation in the Allied armed forces, with pictures of women in uniform engaged in military exercises. Activists quickly adopted the wartime rhetoric that emphasized freedom and justice to outline an agenda for achieving greater equality for Mexican women. They called for jobs in industry and agriculture, protection for women workers through the labor code, greater access to education and training, and a greater voice in the government's economic policies. The demand for women's suffrage was part of the worldwide struggle for democracy. For their part conservative critics challenged feminist arguments by pointing out that women were only performing "masculine" duties because of the wartime exigencies. They expected women to resume their well-defined social and economic roles after the war.

Beauty products appeared in this debate even though retailers hoped to avoid it. Their advertising asserted that wartime changes did not alter notions of femininity and beauty. An advertisement for Pond's face cream claimed that women used the product in defense of liberty. A nail-polish ad declared that "the Modern Woman . . . from the home to the workplace . . . must maintain her femininity: her hands must look beautiful."[10] These new women could be seen in the mass media, such as movie newsreels that showed women on the job dressed in slacks or overalls, or women in new roles, such as parachute nurse (a brigade of which was created by the army). Women found role models in movies and magazines. In 1940 the nation had 466 movie theaters, but that number that expanded to 1,100 by 1946, and the amount spent on entertainment jumped from forty-six million pesos in 1940 to a hundred million during those years, with 80 percent of that amount spent at the movies.[11]

The debate over women's beauty products reached back to more general social divisions created during the Spanish civil war. The reactionary Right, the *sinarquistas* (members of Unión Nacional Sinarquista), saw Franco's victory as the beginning of a worldwide trend. A return to tradition, family, religion, and order appeared imminent. The godless revolutionaries would be driven from power everywhere in the world, including Mexico. The Church wisely dissociated itself from the *sinarquista* movement. As the war began, Germany appeared to be unstoppable as it swept across Europe. When the Japanese attacked Pearl Harbor on December 7, 1941, President Avila Camacho pledged national support to the United States. The decision required a commitment to principle and the reckless hope that the United States could defeat the Axis powers.

As Cárdenes and his cabinet members foresaw, the world crisis resulting from the rise of Nazi Germany, fascist Italy, and imperial Japan accelerated Mexican and United States cooperation. An economic agreement in 1942 lowered tariffs and spelled out the primary products Mexico that could supply, from cotton to ores. Joint military and economic programs were developed, and so were cultural ties. Both nations developed plans for the United States to provide armaments in exchange for a Mexican agreement to patrol the coasts. The Avila Camacho government interned foreign nationals (Germans, Italians, and Japanese) and shared intelligence on enemy activity. Subsequently an expeditionary air force of three hundred Mexicans served in the Philippines and later on Formosa. Some men volunteered for service in the United States armed services through a recruiting station that opened in Mexico City. More than two hundred fifty Mexicans living in the United States enlisted in the army, navy, and marines. In addition Mexican contract workers under the Bracero Program supplied agricultural, factory, and railroad hands. By the end of the war more than half of the *braceros* worked on railroads.

The United States shipped limited supplies of food, some nonessential products, and some railcars south, while Mexicans sent critical raw materials, ranging from lead for bullets to mahogany for PT boat hulls. Agricultural products, especially cottonseed oil used in the war effort, strained Mexico's productive capacity, and food resources were short across the nation as export crops displaced corn, beans, and basic cereals. Only limited supplies could be expected from the United States, partly as a consequence of war demands but also a result of a shortage of boxcars. Some 60 percent of wheat consumed came from U.S. imports, which depended on railroads and the unpredictable supply of equipment. The limited supply of food led to higher prices, panic buying, and hording. Subsidized government retail outlets sold an increasing variety of products. By the war's end 2,500 stores and forty large trucks sold basic items, including milk and eggs.

The government food agency could not service rural areas. The strategy of keeping urban consumers reasonably well supplied left little resources for the countryside. Villagers did the best they could to survive on their own or moved to cities. An estimated four hundred thousand joined the ranks of urban workers. Urban life, for all its adjustment problems, provided a better standard of living than could be expected in small towns and villages. Rural migrants sought what could only be found in the city. Villagers ate daily tortillas, with beans at most two days a week and meat infrequently, while people in the city ate tortillas and beans daily, and meat at least once a week. The switch to the urban foods, especially bread and meat, perhaps mixed with traditional foods, had an impact on energy levels, health, and general well-being. Urban infrastructure required vast financial expenditures but could not catch up with demand. Sewerage in 1939 constituted a serious public health issue. In Oaxaca only 2.8 of the population had access to sewerage systems, while in Morelos a little over 12 percent had service. Mexico City, as to be expected, provided 74.6 percent of its inhabitants with modern sewage disposal.[12]

Agrarian reform withered as urbanization and wartime demands shifted emphasis to commercial production. In 1940, 80 percent of available land grew food crops but three years later that fell to 72 percent. The Avila Camacho administration issued exemptions from land expropriation at over six times the rate of the previous government.[13] Government-funded irrigation projects expanded commercial production. Available credit fell from a per capita 3.2 pesos in 1940 to 1.4 by 1946, much of it financing cotton crops. Private financing of *ejidos* and smaller holdings could not replace federal money. Rural infrastructure, including storage facilities, water, roads, and electrification, never caught up with needs. Secondary schools were not being built at a time when they were most needed. Static landholdings could not support demographic growth. Urban migration or working in the United States became necessary for many. By 1950 some 42.6 percent lived in urban areas and ten years later half of all Mexicans lived in towns and cities.

Inflation cut into wages as urban living costs rose significantly, causing strikes and food riots. The CTM demanded a 50 percent increase in wages. A restructuring of the government food agency could not overcome the lack of production. In 1943, following a poor corn harvest, riots occurred in Mexico City, Monterrey, and elsewhere. People stood in lines all night in the hope of buying corn or followed the word on the street to stores said to have products in short supply. Rumors of widespread corruption and speculation by government officials infuriated desperate consumers.

The end of World War II drew a line between revolutionary and postwar Mexico. A new generation claimed the presidency in 1946.

Suggested Reading

Becker, Marjorie. *Setting the Virgin on Fire: Lázaro Cárdenas, Michoacán Peasants, and the Mexican Revolution*. Berkeley: University of California Press, 1996.

Brown, John C., and Alan Knight, eds. *The Mexican Petroleum Industry in the Twentieth Century*. Austin: University of Texas Press, 1992.

Davis, Diane E. *Urban Leviathan: Mexico City in the Twentieth Century.* Philadelphia: Temple University Press, 1994.
Hershfield, Joanne, and David R. Maciel. *Mexico's Cinema: A Century of Film and Filmmakers.* Wilmington DE: SR Books, 1999.
Niblo, Stephen R. *Mexico in the 1940s: Modernity, Politics, and Corruption.* Wilmington DE: SR Books, 1999.

RECONSTRUCTION OF SOCIETY 

(*Previous page*) 6. Women fleeing to El Paso, Texas. Women fought in the revolution, supported men in battle, or fled—to cities or to exile. Here three women flee to El Paso. Photograph by Otis Aultman. Used with the permission of El Paso Public Library, El Paso, Texas.

During the decades from 1917 to 1946 revolutionaries initiated a variety of campaigns to bring the revolution to the people. These campaigns focused on broadening the reach of existing institutions (schools, for example), redistributing existing resources such as land, and enlarging access to basic needs, including food. At the same time the revolutionaries initiated a campaign that proved to be only partially successful, to remake the symbols of the Porfirian regime in the image of the revolution. Carranza and his followers attempted to remodel cities, not by pulling down statues, wrecking monuments, or destroying the houses of the old regime, but by creating anew. The most obvious and most successful program decorated walls of public buildings. Revolutionary artists painted murals on the facades of edifices built in the Porfirian neoclassical architectural style. The muralists portrayed the revolutionary national history and culture in vivid colors and intense images. In their insurrection, not only did the rebels seize and occupy buildings, they made them their own with paintings of history on the walls.

In other neighborhoods, revolutionaries tore down and remodeled neoclassical homes and built neocolonial ones. They renamed streets, especially after revolutionary martyrs such as Francisco Madero. Public buildings, especially new schools, presented further opportunities to record the names of revolutionary heroes and to emphasize connections between the new regime and the national giants of the past. Above all, the nation's indigenous past was promoted.

Although historians have given much attention to land distribution and labor organization, campaigns to provide adequate food and housing to all Mexicans were equally significant. The housing programs focused especially on shelter for urban migrants. The rising rents made possible by the growing number of residents in cities ultimately resulted in a wave of rent strikes that moved local governments to action. The federal government handled the food supply problem through the creation of a national food agency. Created in 1936, CONASUPO purchased corn, beans, and *chiles*, at first to keep prices down. Soon the agency began to resell products to individuals in Mexico City, and this practice quickly spread other cities and towns. Later, during the 1930s, vans began traveling throughout the countryside with clothing and food to sell at reasonable prices.

The inspiration for the food and rent programs came from Article 29 of the constitution, an article that promised Mexicans a dignified life through sufficient food and adequate housing (at least this is the implication of the antimonopoly provision). Education and work were addressed in other constitutional provisions. Taken together these represent the issues that social revolutionaries worked on during the constructive decades after they came to power.

At the same time the leaders had to confront persistent challenges: the revolutionary military, an aroused Church, (whose leaders included those opposed to revolutionary change but in favor of Catholic social action), regional strongmen, and the aroused people who had expectations based on the revolution's rhetoric.

Another sign of the times appeared in the changed character of the countryside, the scene of revolutionary strife in different locations since November 1910. The most striking change came in the absence of sounds of life. The fighting had reduced animal life, both domestic and wild, and there were fewer human-created sounds, too—the revolutionaries' influence meant less ringing of church bells and fewer religious celebrations (and so less band music and fireworks). The countryside must have become duller, even for those who received land, found railroad union jobs, or attended new schools, with their celebrations and games. Eventually in the 1940s the cacophony returned, especially with the widespread availability of radio, some access to phonographs and records, and a return of church bells, but many rural people had moved to the growing cities, drawn by both economic opportunities and urban excitement.

During the 1920s and 1930s, the revolutionaries had demonstrated their willingness to identify social reforms from other countries, modify them according to circumstances, and try them in Mexico. This open-minded approach made the Mexican Revolution different than the other great revolutions of the century. Of these initiatives inspired by international efforts, none had great significance to the revolutionaries than the program in education. The campaign to create heirs of the revolution through popular education resulted in both urban and rural programs of both formal and informal instruction, reaching adults and children of indigenous and *mestizo* heritage. Minister of Public Education José Vasconcelos laid the groundwork for this program that received particular emphasis from Plutarco E. Calles who declared: "The children are the revolution."

A sampling of the reactions of children to the revolutionary programs comes from the government-published *Pulgarcito*, a children's magazine that printed drawings, essays, and letters. *Pulgarcito* was one of many popular media for children, along with radio and theater. These allowed children the chance to voice their views of the revolutionary society. Children's drawings received international circulation through a competition held in conjunction with the 1927 Geneva Convention on the Rights of the Child, and other international exhibitions. The exchange of drawings between Mexican and Japanese children resulted in the publication by a Japanese company of a run of thirty thousand postcards of the Mexican drawings. The goal of these efforts, beyond encouraging youth creativity, was the creation and fostering of a sense of revolutionary nationalism.[1]

The Middle Class Rising

The years from 1938 to 1946 included the end of the Cárdenas presidency (1938–1940), World War II, the rise of import substitution economics, migration to Mexico City, and flagrant public corruption. These years have been examined by historians from all of these perspectives, but can best be considered as ones in which the middle class identified themselves as the revolution's heirs. A policy shift resulted in 1937–1938 enhanced programs for the urban population. The revolutionary rhetoric had focused on the countryside, with land, education, and religious reforms, and incorporation of the indigenous peoples into the national population. Labor policies in the cities had remained a distant second in emphasis; most union interest occurred in rural areas with the remote oil camps, mining settlements, and nomadic railroad workers. And the muralists with their public art, intellectuals, folk artists, artisans, and novelists, all had found the nation's essence in the rural community. So it was a curious matter that the revolution that had begun in the countryside and which had focused on rural programs until 1937 shifted its emphasis to the city.

This new era emerged under the direction of Lázaro Cárdenas. In 1937 the president abandoned the redistributive revolution and moved to a program intended to increase production so that society would have more to distribute. This developmental revolution relied on the intervention of the national government in the economy and its management to insure increased production. The move to central government management of the economy received dramatic initiation when Cárdenas expropriated the petroleum industry. He established a government corporation to replace foreign drilling and production companies and to create a refining and distribution corporation.

The nationalistic revolution developed programs to benefit the *mestizo* middle class. The catchwords of the early revolution—land reform, labor rights, and food for all—shifted to new ones: health reform, "Made in Mexico," and moral behavior. Middle-class citizens living in cities, especially the capital, held professional jobs, including ones in law, education, medicine, and the government. For the most part they had careers that required educational degrees. President Avila Camacho's wife, Soledad, reflected middle-class conservatism, demanding that the new statue of Diana on Reforma Avenue have a loincloth covering her pubic area. Sporadic campaigns against the alleged financial corruption of government officials, including presidents after they left office, sought to appease middle-class outrage.

Certainly one measure of the revolutionaries' success can be recalled in government-sponsored media. The national government inspired what some Mexicans today recall as the Golden Age of movies, radio, and popular music. The success of these popular industries rested squarely on the government's encouragement and financial assistance. A government bank invested directly in some feature films and provided indirect financing of movie studios that produced classic films, starring Dolores del Rio, Pedro Armendariz, comic Cantinflas, and musical performers Jose Alfredo Jímenez, Pedro Infante, and Jorge Negrete.

Popular music became increasingly widespread through radio broadcasts of both live and recorded performances by the likes of Jímenez, Infante, and Negrete. Equally important was the government's involvement in the record industry, especially financing recording studios and record distribution.

Radio received double attention from the central government. The Cárdenas administration distributed radio receivers to remote villages throughout its regime and successfully used radio to broadcast reports to a national audience of all of Cárdenas's major actions, such as the expropriation of the petroleum industry. Cárdenas created the same sense of intimacy with listeners that President Franklin D. Roosevelt had done in the United States with his "fireside chats." Second, the government used *The National Hour* (*La Hora Nacional*) each Sunday evening to promote the regime and its view of the revolution. A law initiated in 1932 required that all stations air the program or suspend broadcasting.

The program included national reports, music, folklore, and descriptions of the nation's geography and peoples. At times the announcements focused on spectacular geographic or archaeological sites, to promote tourism within the country and to familiarize the listeners with their country's treasures. Initially the program was broadcast under the auspices of the Ministry of Education, clearly revealing its pedagogical goals. But heavy-handed doses of nationalistic and pedantic educational programs resulted in widespread satire of *La Hora Nacional.* A succession of directors tinkered with the variety of features on the program, but more and more Mexican tunes and literary readings—rather than educational ones—filled the program. The political segments simply disappeared.

Radio, movies, and records found an eager audience in towns and across the countryside. Mexicans enjoyed movies in Art Deco theaters and on bedsheet screens, played the latest recorded music on electricity- or battery-powered Victrolas, and listened to radios everywhere. Despite the tremendous popularity, not all were happy with this. Perhaps the most vocal, certainly the most tenacious were those who organized the Association of Catholic Parents to demand censorship.

Middle-class preferences shaped the newly emerging urban culture and identified major concerns. Order, propriety, and industry became the watchwords. This brought a focus on creating a sense of safety in the city. If crime, morality, and unhealthy activity could not be eliminated, it could be reduced, regulated, and removed from view. This resulted in the daylight rise of leisure activities regarded as appropriate, healthful, entertaining relief from the daily grind—namely sports. Soccer especially but also baseball became a popular pastimes and spectator attractions.

Because of their mass audiences, radio and movies attracted middle-class campaigns aimed at insuring propriety. This meant punishing the guilty and immoral, and rewarding the innocent and moral. These campaigns, along with one to regulate the highly popular comic books, never completely succeeded but the effort resulted in self-censorship within the industry.

Mexico City nightlife now had a different character, centered at a variety of new locations. For the elites, new nightclubs combined fancy restaurants, dance floors, and musical reviews in chic locations. Inspired by the Moulin Rouge in Paris and New York City's Rainbow Ballroom, Ciros (in the Reforma Hotel) and the Versailles Room (in the Del Prado Hotel) attracted the celebrities of the mass media, movie, radio, and recording personalities who added glitter to the experience of dinner, dancing, and enjoying live radio broadcasts. Hollywood stars, national politicians, musical celebrities, and successful artists rubbed shoulders and shared the dance floor. They drank, danced, and dressed just like high society in Paris, London, and New York. The cosmopolitan character of the nightclubs could be seen clearly in the most popular drinks. Scotch and bourbon remained most popular, followed by various mixed drinks, especially the Big Bertha (tequila and simple syrup), but the margarita had not yet been invented. The middle class could not afford to become regulars, but they could splurge for a special occasion at these clubs.

The lower classes had new attractions at night as well, with the rise of dance halls (referred to as cabarets) that featured live or recorded music, the latest dances, and young women—*cabareteras*—who served as partners in exchange for tickets. These women became the subject of mournful ballads and mawkish films. Often these girls came from the countryside and found jobs dancing. Many, through desperation or naiveté, slipped into prostitution. For both the upper and middle classes, these cabarets had the attraction of the exotic and the hint of underworld danger that prompted people to go slumming.

Populist leaders, people such as Cárdenas, had given new attention to working-class people in order to attract their political support, often identifying their cultural practices as being the authentic national culture. In this way popular culture increasingly became the national culture, embraced by everyone to the point that it even became a commodity to be offered to foreign tourists visiting Mexico City. In real ways the capital (as with other large cities) became two cities in one location, one by day, another by night. Each had a geography, energy, and population of its own. To some extent radio became the bridge between classes, the radio that beamed music and interviews from nightclubs to the homes of eager listeners. These two societies, one of the day and the other of the night, did not suddenly appear in 1938 and expand over the next decade. Rather they represented the culmination of changes emanating from the 1920s. These precursory events can be summed up by looking at city planning and urban architecture. During the decades from 1917 to 1938, when revolutionary leaders focused on the redistributive rural revolution, urban centers were little more than big villages. The tallest building in the capital stood only three stories and the city offered few conveniences beyond those available in the countryside. Erratic electricity, spotty sewerage, and sputtering trolley cars began to change all that in the 1930s, with dramatic, tall buildings creating urban canyons, traffic jams of buses and trucks, and a sonic explosion of radio and car horns. The familiarity of neighbors and the desire for handmade tortillas gave way as respect for the land eroded and Mexicans became city people.

Revolutionary leaders, especially the presidents, seized on the emerging urban culture and used it to create populist politics. The presidents promoted and associated with mariachi bands, appeared in public with radio and movie stars, and changed the lyrics of popular songs to support their election.

Suggested Reading

Benjamin, Thomas. *La Revolución: Mexico's Great Revolution as Memory, Myth and History*. Austin: University of Texas Press, 2000.

Knight, Alan. "Popular Culture and the Revolutionary State in Mexico, 1910–1940," *Hispanic American Historical Review* 74, no. 3 (August 1994): 393–444.

Turner, Frederick C. *The Dynamic of Mexican Nationalism*. Chapel Hill: University of North Carolina Press, 1968.

Wilkie, James W. *The Mexican Revolution: Federal Expenditure and Social Change Since 1910*, 2nd rev. ed. Berkeley: University of California Press, 1970.

CONCLUSION

Reflections on the Mexican Revolution

(*Previous page*) 7. Women revolutionaries in Mexico City. Female soldier (*una soldana*). Women participated in the revolution as soldiers and served as commissary and medical aides. Here one of the female revolutionaries moves on campaign, demonstrating the active participation of both men and women in the struggle for social change. Photograph by Otis Aultman, used with permission of the El Paso Public Library, El Paso, Texas.

A generation of men and women made the revolution in Mexico. For the most part they dismissed utopian visions as they gave their attention to hard-nosed practical programs that benefited the people they knew. As their fundamental goal they sought an immediate improvement in their own lives and the lives of their compatriots, regardless of geography, race, language, or occupation, without distinctions between rural and urban populations. Revolution demanded immediate action and concrete change. Villagers on the march underscored their demands with bullets. This ideology of action had a pragmatic character based on location—a need to confront local problems first.

These revolutionaries found inspiration in some of their nation's previous values and objectives that had never been realized. They looked to the Constitution of 1857 and its anticlericalism became a part of their program. They did not start out with the Church as a target but it became one when it intervened in national, political, and social issues. The incorporation of the anticlerical provisions of the Constitution of 1857 in the Constitution of 1917 reinvigorated the issue through the 1930s. The anticlericalism in Tabasco under Tomás Garrido Canabal represented the extreme, while the socialist education campaign, for all the fury vented against it by the Church, represented a mild alternative. The federal government bureaucrats could not decide what "socialist education" even meant and, beyond the name, could not control the practice of village schoolteachers.

The continuity expressed by the incorporation of elements of 1857 in the 1917 Constitution made it possible to revise rather than demolish the existing government. Francisco Madero, Venustiano Carranza, Alvaro Obregón, and every president—elected and provisional—functioned within the same basic institutional and bureaucratic structure created after the 1867 defeat of the French. The one exception: the discharge of the federal army resulting from the 1914 Treaty of Teoloyucan following the removal of the Huerta regime. Even then the revolutionary army reincorporated many of the lower elements of the old army, becoming a revolutionary institution. The army would be employed to incorporate revolutionary generals in a largely successful effort to control them.

Revolutionaries understood that force provided the initial entry into power but that politics within the established institutional structure supplied legitimacy. Nevertheless leaders needed battlefield experience. General Alvaro Obregón represented the ideal revolutionary general: undefeated, willing to risk his life to confront the enemy, and—most impressively—a natural tactician. Only the most reckless considered opposing him, on or off the battlefield. Creation of the PNR—and subsequently the PRM as the governing party—reduced the violence of political campaigns and the need for army intervention.

Revolutionaries responded to the demands of land-hungry peasants but they tried to balance these with the commercialization of agriculture for urban food demands and critical export revenues. The new constituency of urban workers also claimed their attention. The combination of urban food needs and other urban political pressures ultimately would shift the emphasis away from agrarian reforms. Land reform, road building, bus service, and school programs did much to improve life in the countryside, but the needs of urban workers posed a more difficult challenge. Many of these first-generation city dwellers made their claims for attention as veterans of the revolution and strengthened their demands through unions. The CROM, an umbrella organization of many different unions, under the direction of Luis Morones, and the CTM, under the leadership Vicente Lombardo Toledano, both were groups that the president and other political leaders had to reckon with. The government used workers as a tool to intimidate employers and to make deals with them over wages and labor conditions. Politicians manipulated the definition of a legal strike for administrative needs.

The revolutionaries who crafted programs that represented the needs and concerns of their people also demonstrated a receptivity toward foreign programs of reform that had succeeded. Revolutionary representatives traveled widely, in both official and unofficial capacities, in search of programs, institutions, and organizations that worked for the betterment of people. This openness makes Mexicans stand out among other revolutionaries of the century.

Many of the achievements of the revolution were obscured by events beginning in 1946, when a second generation of revolutionaries came to power. Renamed the Party of the Institutionalized Revolution, the party and government administration would go on to cynically practice political manipulation, engage in corrupt financial deals, and oversee repression and injustice for the rest of the century, as society experienced a growing disparity of wealth. These failures do not dismiss the successes of the revolutionary generation that successfully established a regime and carried out revolutionary policies from 1910 to 1946.

The emergence of a government held responsible for positive change for ordinary citizens underpins legitimacy. The people demanded respect across the board, radical change, and positive action to make life better both in the short and long run. They demanded economic security, expressed in demands for land and village improvements, and subsequently labor protection and safety-net institutions, such as social security and public health programs. The transformation of the countryside resulted in the creation of a fluid rural population better able to contend with demands on its land and labor. For example, government credit agencies broke the monopoly of local money leaders for the first time. Those able to use the rails and new roads had much-improved economic possibilities, with the option of moving to the cities. Rural isolation gave way to national inclusion. Children learned to read and write in modest schools, beginning a process that would eventually take their children and grandchildren to secondary schools, professional institutes, and universities.

Social stratification underwent fundamental changes leading to a class system, with the possibility of upward mobility. The displacement of the elites during the revolution opened political positions at the national and state level to a generation of revolutionaries, largely from the middle and lower classes. Closely coupled with social change, the revolution proudly elevated Indian Mexico to be a part of the national uniqueness. The revolutionary ideal rested on the national culture cleansed of its negative elements. Respect and pride made it possible to use nationalism to bind the republic and classes together.

The revolution did not resolve all the problems that confronted the people in 1910. Moreover it faced new problems as the nation became more industrial and moved further away from subsistence agriculture. These difficulties resulted in the challenges of the second half of the twentieth century. Typical of popular movements, the revolutionary institutions—the government and the party—that had done so much from 1910 to 1946, became the obstacles to the resolution of the new challenges from 1946 to 2000. What the revolutionary party and government became after 1946 cannot diminish the fact that a generation of everyday Mexican citizens made the world's first social revolution.

The second generation of revolutionaries came to power with the election of Miguel Alemán in 1946. These sons and daughters of the veterans of revolutionary battles had come of age in entirely different circumstances. A sweeping generalization about the generation of revolutionaries identifies their rough-hewn, self-made character. Generally they lacked much schooling and they relied on the education of practical experience and learning gained by surviving violence. Even the most successful of them retained small-town, provincial values. They had attempted to educate the young of their families and nation to be revolutionaries.

Some of the heirs of the revolutionary veterans lived the improved life that their predecessors wanted for them, although many did not. Generally the new revolutionary generation had been reared in affluence, received extensive schooling, and been encouraged into the professions. Living in large cities, many in the capital itself, they had an urban orientation with both a disregard for the countryside and an apprehension about city life that appeared in the popular arts and media. Although they knew the myths and rhetoric of their parents' achievements, once they took charge of the nation they acted—in many ways—as strangers in the land of revolution.

NOTES

2. The New Generation and Revolution Change

1. Gretchen Pierce, "Sober Revolutionaries: Ethnicity, Class, and Gender in Jalisco, Oaxaca, and Sonora, Mexico, 1910–1940," unpublished PhD diss., University of Arizona, 2008.

2. Quoted in John W. F. Dulles, *Yesterday in Mexico: A Chronicle of the Revolution, 1919–1936* (Austin: University of Texas Press, 1961), 299.

3. Pope John Paul II beatified Father Pro in 1988.

4. Alicia Azuela de la Cueva, *Arte y Poder: Renacimento Artístico y Revolución Social, Mexico, 1910–1945* (Zamora, Mich.: El Colegio de Michoacan: Fondo de Cultura Económica, 2005), 275–328.

3. Reelection and Contested Suffrage

1. Mejía Barquera F., *La Industria de la Radio y Television y la Política del Estado Mexicano (1920–1960)* (Mexico City: Fundacíon Manuel Buendía, 1989), 51, and Joy Elizabeth Hayes, *Radio Nation: Communication, Culture, and Nationalism in Mexico, 1920–1950* (Tucson: University of Arizona Press, 2000), 39.

2. Josephus Daniels, *Shirt-Sleeve Diplomat* (Chapel Hill: University of North Carolina Press, 1947), 51.

3. Several years earlier, in 1928, Mexico rejected the appointment of a military attaché because of his service in the Veracruz occupation force. Just a month before the government had decorated surviving Mexican defenders. Apparently his close connection with FDR made the difference (Cronon, 15).

4. As secretary of the navy he appointed a Catholic as the chief of operations, increased the number of Catholic navy chaplains, and supported Al Smith in the 1928 presidential race. E. David Cronin, *Josephus Daniels in Mexico* (Madison: University of Wisconsin Press, 1960), 15.

5. The Scopes trial in Tennessee in 1925, also known as "the Monkey Trial,"

pitted evolution against the Bible in a contest that engaged most of the world. It had an undetermined influence on plans for scientific socialist education.

4. Lázaro Cárdenas in Power

1. Angela Villalba, *Mexican Calendar Girls* (San Francisco: Chronicle Books, 2006).

2. Roderic Camp, *General in the Palacio: The Military in Modern Mexico* (New York: Oxford University Press, 1992), 44, 418.

3. Roderic A. Camp, *Mexican Political Biographies, 1935–1976* (Tucson: University of Arizona Press, 1976), 36–37.

4. James C. Helfley, *Adáron Sáenz: Mexico's Revolutionary Capitalist* (Waco TX: Word Books, 1970).

5. Francisco E. Balderama and Raymond Rodríguez, *Decade of Betrayal: Mexican Repatriation in the 1930s* (Albuquerque: University of New Mexico Press, 1995), 99.

6. Balderama and Rodríguez observed that in the 1930s both governments considered anyone of Mexican descent to be Mexican, whether naturalized or born in the United States. Balderama and Rodríguez, *Decade of Betrayal*, 111–212. Today class-action suits by these citizens forced out of the country are under consideration.

5. The Tipping Point

1. Enrique C. Ochoa, *Feeding Mexico: The Political Uses of Food since 1910* (Wilmington DE: Scholarly Resources, 2000), 44–52.

2. Stephen R. Niblo, *Mexico in the 1940s: Modernity, Politics, and Corruption* (Wilmington DE: Scholarly Resources, 1999), 86.

3. Friedrich E. Schuler, *Mexico between Hitler and Roosevelt: Mexican Foreign Policy in the Age of Lázaro Cárdenas, 1934–1940* (Albuquerque: University of New Mexico Press, 1998), 181–90.

4. Franz A. von Sauer, *The Alienated "Loyal" Opposition: Mexico's Partido Accion Nacional* (Albuquerque: University of New Mexico Press, 1974), 26.

5. Both quotes in Betty Kirk, *Covering the Mexican Front: The Battle of Europe versus America* (Norman: University of Oklahoma Press, 1942), 330.

6. Gregg Andrews, *Shoulder to Shoulder: The American Federation of Labor, the United States and the Mexican Revolution* (Berkeley: University of California Press), 68.

7. Kevin J. Middlebrook, *The Paradox of Revolution: Labor, the State, and Authoritarianism in Mexico* (Baltimore MD: Johns Hopkins University Press, 1995), 70.

8. Rose J. Spalding, "Social Security Policy Making: The Formation and Evolution of the Mexican Social Security Institute," unpublished PhD diss., University of North Carolina, Chapel Hill, 1978.

9. Jeffrey M. Pilcher, *Cantinflas and the Chaos of Mexican Modernity* (Wilmington DE: Scholarly Resources, 2001), xxii.

10. Monica Rankin, "Feminism vs. Feminine: Gender Roles in Public Spaces in 1940s Mexico." Presentation at the American Historical Association Annual Meeting, January 2008.

11. Carl Mora, *Mexican Cinema: Reflections on a Society, 1896–1988*, 2nd ed. (Berkeley: University of California Press, 1988), 20.

12. James W. Wilkie, *The Mexican Revolution: Federal Expenditure and Social Change Since 1910* (Berkeley: University of California Press, 1967), 204–45.

13. Ochoa, *Feeding Mexico*, 72.

6. Reconstruction of Society

1. Elena J. Albarrán, "Children of the Revolution: Constructing the Mexican Citizen, 1920–1940," unpublished PhD diss., University of Arizona, 2007.

TWENTY-FIVE OUTSTANDING BOOKS ON REVOLUTIONARY MEXICO

Classic and General Accounts

1. Charles C. Cumberland. *The Mexican Revolution: The Constitutional Years.* Austin: University of Texas Press, 1972.
2. Alan Knight. *The Mexican Revolution.* New York: Cambridge University Press, 1986.
3. John M. Hart. *Revolutionary Mexico: The Coming and Process of the Mexican Revolution.* Berkeley: University of California Press, 1989.
4. Frank Tannenbaum. *Mexico: The Struggle for Peace and Bread.* New York: Alfred A. Knopf, 1950.
5. John W. F. Dulles. *Yesterday in Mexico: A Chronicle of the Revolution, 1919–1936.* Austin: University of Texas Press, 1961.
6. Anita Benner. *The Wind that Swept Mexico: The History of the Mexican Revolution, 1910*–1942. Austin: University of Texas Press, 1971.
7. Ernest Gruening. *Mexico and Its Heritage.* New York: Appleton-Century-Crofts, 1928.
8. James Wilkie. *The Mexican Revolution: Federal Expenditure and Social Change since 1910.* Berkeley: University of California Press, 1967.

Biographies

9. William H. Beezley. *Insurgent Governor: Abraham González and the Mexican Revolution.* Lincoln: University of Nebraska Press, 1972.
10. Charles C. Cumberland. *The Mexican Revolution: The Genesis Under Madero.* Austin: University of Texas Press, 1952.
11. Friedrich Katz. *The Life and Times of Pancho Villa.* Stanford CA: Stanford University Press, 1998.
12. Michael C. Meyer. *Huerta: A Political Portrait.* Lincoln: University of Nebraska Press, 1972.

13. Jurgen Buchenau. *Plutarco Elías Calles and the Mexican Revolution.* Lanham MD: Rowman and Littlefield, 2006.
14. John Womack. *Zapata and the Mexican Revolution.* New York: Alfred A. Knopf, 1969.
15. Douglas Richmond. *Venustiano Carranza's Nationalist Struggle, 1893–1920.* Lincoln: University of Nebraska Press, 1983.

Assessments of Revolutionary Programs and Challengers

16. David C. Bailey. *¡Viva Cristo Rey! The Cristero Rebellion and the Church-State Conflict in Mexico.* Austin: University of Texas Press, 1974.
17. Katherine E. Bliss. *Compromised Positions: Prostitution, Public Health, and Gender Politics in Revolutionary Mexico.* University Park: Pennsylvania State University Press, 2001.
18. Susie S. Porter. *Working Women in Mexico City: Public Discourses and Material Conditions, 1879–1931.* Tucson: University of Arizona Press, 2003.
19. Adrian A. Bantjes. *As If Jesus Walked on Earth: Cardenismo, Sonora, and the Mexican Revolution.* Wilmington DE: SR Books, 1998.
20. Mary Kay Vaughan. *Cultural Politics in Revolution: Teachers, Peasants, and Schools in Mexico, 1930–1940.* Tucson: University of Arizona Press, 1997.
21. Christopher Boyer. *Becoming Campesino: Politics, Identity, and Agrarian Struggle in Michoacán, 1920–1935.* Stanford CA: Stanford University Press, 2003.
22. John Lear. *Workers, Neighbors, and Citizens: The Revolution in Mexico City.* Lincoln: University of Nebraska Press, 2001.
23. Ilene V. O'Malley. *The Myth of the Revolution: Hero Cults and the Institutionalization of the Mexican Revolution, 1920*–1940. Westport CT: Greenwood Press, 1986.
24. Thomas Benjamin. *La Revolución: Mexico's Great Revolution as Memory, Myth, and History.* Austin: University of Texas Press, 2000.
25. Dina Berger. *The Development of Mexico's Tourist Industry: Pyramids by Day, Martinis by Night.* New York: Palgrave Macmillan, 2006.

INDEX

Page numbers in italic refer to illustrations

In the Mexican Experience series

Mexicans in Revolution, 1910–1946: An Introduction
William H. Beezley and Colin M. MacLachlan

Forceful Negotiations: The Origins of the Pronunciamiento *in Nineteenth-Century Mexico*
Edited and with an introduction by Will Fowler

Malcontents, Rebels, and Pronunciados: *The Politics of Insurrection in Nineteenth-Century Mexico*
Edited and with an introduction by Will Fowler

Gender and the Negotiation of Daily Life in Mexico, 1750–1856
Sonya Lipsett-Rivera

Mexico's Crucial Century, 1810–1910: An Introduction
Colin M. MacLachlan and William H. Beezley

¡México, la patria! Propaganda and Production during World War II
Monica A. Rankin

Pistoleros and Popular Movements: The Politics of State Formation in Postrevolutionary Oaxaca
Benjamin T. Smith

To order or obtain more information on these or other
University of Nebraska Press titles, visit www.nebraskapress.unl.edu.

CPSIA information can be obtained
at www.ICGtesting.com
Printed in the USA
LVOW13s2015200717
542040LV00017B/225/P

THE MEXICAN EXPERIENCE

On November 20, 1910, Mexicans initiated the world's first popular social revolution. The unbalanced progress of the previous regime triggered violence and mobilized individuals from all classes to demand social and economic justice. In the process they shaped modern Mexico at a cost of two million lives.

This accessible and gripping account guides the reader through the intricacies of the revolution, focusing on the revolutionaries as a group and the implementation of social and political changes. In this volume written for the revolution's centennial, William H. Beezley and Colin M. MacLachlan recount how the revolutionary generation laid the foundation for a better life for all Mexicans.

William H. Beezley is a professor of history at the University of Arizona. He is the author or editor of dozens of books, including *Judas at the Jockey Club and Other Episodes of Porfirian Mexico*, 2nd ed., available in a Bison Books edition, and is the coeditor of *The Oxford History of Mexico.*

Colin M. MacLachlan is the John Christie Barr Distinguished Professor of History at Tulane University. He has written numerous historical works, including *Spain's Empire in America: The Role of Ideas in Institutional and Social Change* and *Anarchism and the Mexican Revolution: The Political Trials of Ricardo Flores Magón in the United States.*

Cover: *Calaveras de la revolucion* by Mauricio Hernández Colmenero. From the Champion Folkart Colllection, Tucson, Arizona. Photograph by Cheryle Champion.

ISBN 978-0-8032-2447-6

9 780803 224476

University of Nebraska Press
Lincoln NE 68588-0630
www.nebraskapress.unl.edu